อาหารกับแกล้ม

pokpok

THE DRINKING FOOD OF THAILAND

อาหารกับแกล้ม

pok pok

THE DRINKING FOOD OF THAILAND

ANDY RICKER WITH JJ GOODE

Photography by Austin Bush

TEN SPEED PRESS
California | New York

CONTENTS

Introduction 1

About This Book 6

Using a Mortar and Pestle 9

Lao Khao: Rice whiskey 11

KHAWNG WAANG: SNACKS

Kai Saam Yang: Chicken three ways 20

Plaa Lek Thawt Krob: Fried tiny fish 23

Thua Thawt Samun Phrai: Fried peanuts with makrut lime leaves, garlic, and chiles 26

Kung Ten: Dancing shrimp 29

Plaa Meuk Ping: Grilled dried cuttlefish 32

Phrik Kleua: Salt-chile dip for green mango 35

Yam Met Mamuang Himaphaan: Fried cashews with salt, chiles, and green onions 37

Ya Dawng: Herbal rice whiskey 40

TOM: SOUP

Kaeng Awm Neua: Northern Thai stewed beef 45

Yam Kop: Northern Thai frog soup 49

Tom Saep Muu: Isaan sour soup with pork 52

Tom Som Kai Baan: Sour Northern Thai "village chicken" soup 57

NAAM PHRIK: CHILE DIPS

Naam Phrik Taa Daeng: Red-eye chile dip 63

Naam Phrik Khaa: Galangal chile dip 67

Naam Phrik Num: Green chile dip 71

Bia: Beer 73

KHAWNG THAWT: FRIED FOODS

Laap Muu Thawt: Fried minced pork patties 79

Sai Muu / Huu Muu Thawt: Fried chitterlings / pig's ears 84

En Kai Thawt: Fried chicken tendons 88

Neua / Muu Daet Diaw: Fried semidried beef / pork 91

Kai Thawt: Thai-style fried chicken 95

Som Tam Thawt: Fried papaya salad 101

Khaep Muu: Pork cracklings 107

Naem Sii Khrong Muu: Fried sour pork ribs 109

Muu Yaang Thawt: Fried grilled pork 115

Mam: Isaan beef and liver sausage 117

Sii Khrong Muu Tai Naam: Pork ribs cooked "underwater" 124

KHAWNG YAANG: GRILLED FOODS

A note on Thai grilling 129

Jin Tup: Hammered flank steak 135

BBQ: Thai-style barbecue beef skewers 137

Aep Samoeng Muu: Pig's brains grilled in banana leaf 141

Hang Muu Yaang: Grilled pig's tails 144

Sai Krawk Isaan: Isaan fermented pork-and-rice sausages 147

Tap Kai / Tap Pet Ping: Grilled chicken / duck liver skewers 153

Kung Phao: Grilled prawns 157

Jin Som Mok Khai: Sour pork and egg grilled in banana leaves 158

Whiskey Soda 162

YAM: SALADS

Sup Naw Mai: Isaan bamboo shoot salad 166

Yam Plaa Meuk: Squid salad 172

Yam Plaa Salit: Fried gouramy fish salad 174

Yam Wun Sen: Glass noodle salad 177

Yam Mama: Instant-noodle salad 180

Yam Het Huu Nuu Khao: Mouse ear mushroom salad 184

Tap Waan: Isaan pork liver salad 187

Laap Neua Dip: Nan-style minced raw beef "salad" 188

Laap Phrae: Phrae-style minced pork "salad" 192

KHAWNG PHAT: STIR-FRIES

Phat Khii Mao: Drunkard's stir-fry 201

Khua Haem Pik Kai: Stir-fried chicken wings with hot basil and chiles 205

Phat Hoi Laai Samun Phrai: Stir-fried clams with krachai, galangal, and Thai basil 209

KHAWNG KIN RAWP DEUK / KHAWNG KIN CHAO: LATE-NIGHT AND MORNING FOOD

Khao Tom: Rice soup 214

Jok: Rice porridge 217

Tom Leuat Muu: Pork soup with steamed blood cakes and offal 219

Kuaytiaw Luuk Chin Plaa Hua Nom: Noodle soup with tiny fish balls 223

Muu Ping: Grilled pork skewers 226

Khai Luak Kap Khanom Pang Ping: Thai-style coddled eggs with toast 229

SUNDRY ITEMS

Khao Khua: Toasted–sticky rice powder 232

Phrik Pon Khua: Toasted-chile powder 233

Krathiam Jiaw and Naam Man Krathiam: Fried garlic and garlic oil 234

Hom Jiaw and Naam Man Hom Jiaw: Fried shallots and shallot oil 235

Naam Makham Piak: Tamarind water 236

Naam Cheuam Naam Taan Piip: Palm sugar simple syrup 237

Kapi Kung: Homemade shrimp paste 238

Kung Haeng Khua: Dry-fried dried shrimp 239

Naam Boon Sai: Limestone water 240

Sup Kraduuk Muu: Thai pork stock 241

Naam Jim Seafood: Spicy, tart dipping sauce for seafood 243

Naam Jim Kai: Sweet chile dipping sauce 244

Jaew: Isaan dipping sauce 245

Muu Deng: Bouncy pork balls 246

Khao Hom Mali: Jasmine rice 247

Khao Niaw: Sticky rice 248

Ingredients 251

Equipment 257

Acknowledgments 258

Index 260

INTRODUCTION

Long before I opened Pok Pok, before I even knew there was such a thing as "Northern Thai food," I learned a lesson about drinking in Thailand.

I was on Ko Tao, now a destination for divers, but in the mid-1980s, a more or less deserted island in the Gulf of Thailand—just a coconut plantation and a few bungalows. I had planned to stay for a matter of days, but three months later, I still hadn't left. I got stuck there, like so many people do, ensnared by white sand, postcard-worthy turquoise water, and a strong dollar. Only when I lost my contact lenses did I lift myself off a hammock and buy a ticket on the coconut boat heading toward the mainland to re-up.

At the time, you could purchase cheap passage on a fishing boat whose hull was heaped with coconuts. I, along with a motley bunch of tourists and Thais, sat on the tarp thrown over the fruits as the boat chugged toward the fishing town of Chumphon, where I'd catch a fourteen-hour, eighty-baht (a little over a dollar at the time) bus to Bangkok. The ride was uneventful until I got a tap on the shoulder. I clicked off my Walkman and turned to an Australian guy who said matter-of-factly, "Mate, you've got a scorpion on your head." Freaked, I dipped my head, the giant creature fell, and my savior squashed it with his sandal—or, as he'd have called it, his thong.

In Chumphon, I boarded a bus crammed with Thais, mostly squid fishermen, with three per bench seat and just enough legroom for a toddler. At the time, the sight of a foreigner (*farang*) was a relative novelty. Blond-haired and six feet two, I was quite the sight wedged into a seat. I could speak almost no Thai back then, just "hello" and "thank you." No one on the bus spoke more than a few words of English. Despite the language barrier, a group of smiling guys sitting near me got my attention, waving two bottles and calling, "You, you!" To pass the time on the long ride, they were taking shots of Mekhong (a sort of hectic Thai rum) and chasing it with Lipovitan, a Japanese-made precursor to Red Bull ubiquitous in Thailand at the time. They wanted me to join, and I figured, why not? Two hours later, after a lot of laughing and slapping one another on the back, the bus made a pit stop. The lot of us stumbled out single file—squid fisherman, squid fisherman, squid fisherman, white guy—to take a piss, and the whole bus erupted in laughter and rowdy calls of "*farang*! *farang*!"

That wasn't the last time I would befriend strangers over drinks. A frequent traveler to Thailand over the past two decades, I've been waved over countless times at restaurants and pubs and invited to partake in someone else's booze. I've been flagged down in alleys to take up residence at impromptu bars—maybe miniature stools pulled up to a repurposed ice chest draped with oilcloth— and share unlabeled spirits, like *ya dawng* and *lao saparot*, rice liquors flavored with, respectively, medicinal herbs and pineapple. I've had arms thrown around me at karaoke bars by the wasted and merry, who then proceeded to fill my glass again and again from tall bottles of beer. Early on, before I made true friends in Thailand, these booze-fueled interactions were essentially my only opportunities to go beyond the tourist experience, to interact with Thai people, to feel their warmth and inclusiveness.

And because this was Thailand, where food is ever present, I often ate with my new friends, too. These weren't full-on meals, however. Instead, my comrades-for-the-night introduced me to a subset of the cuisine, little known in the States, called *aahaan kap klaem*, or "drinking food."

In Thailand, you almost never see people drinking without *something* to eat. I have yet to enter a Thai establishment where there's booze but no food on offer. That impromptu alley bar, for example, might have set out drinking fare at its most basic: small bowls of *mayom*, a tiny, bracingly tart fruit not unlike a crab apple, or salty fermented shrimp paste to be eaten by the pinch. At a roadside pub outside of Chiang Mai, friends down beers and eat *jin tup*, marinated flank steak grilled way past medium-rare, pounded to shreds with a sledgehammer, and eaten with a dip made from dried chile and galangal. In the Northeast of Thailand, glasses of "whiskey" empty steadily around a pot of *tom saep khwai*, incendiary soup packed with water buffalo offal and seasoned with lime and various rhizomes and herbs, from which everyone takes spoonfuls between slugs. At someone's home, an ingenious cook might use a wok set over a charcoal fire to turn stonelike tamarind seeds, without pulp, into a crunchy snack.

No hard-and-fast definition of drinking food exists, no list of dishes that you eat only when you're drinking. In another context, many examples of *aahaan kap klaem* would certainly wind up on the table at a proper dinner, alongside other dishes and heaps of rice (see "About This Book," page 6). It's true, too, that there are few dishes you *wouldn't* have a drink with, if you felt like it. But just as America has salted peanuts, Buffalo wings, and nachos, Thais have a particular roster—and a particularly vast and exciting one—of dishes that are closely associated with drinking that I've seen again and again at the bars, karaoke joints, dance halls, cabarets, and other watering holes of Thailand over the past two decades. Like the American category, the dishes of *aahaan kap klaem* share certain characteristics. Often insistently spicy, salty, chewy, and/ or sour, they're meant to keep you drinking, to keep the night going.

Many years after my Mekhong-fueled bus ride, I opened a place in Portland called Whiskey Soda Lounge. I named it for the Thai cocktail of choice: a bottle of "whisk-EE" (a generic term for hard brown liquor) and its nearly inseparable partner, "so-DAH." It was supposed to be a holding pen for customers waiting for a table at Pok Pok, across the street. But once people wrapped their heads around the concept—a bar with the sort of spicy, sour, salty food you'd find in Thailand but you don't typically see in this part of the world—Whiskey Soda Lounge became a destination in its own right.

Just as Whiskey Soda Lounge is as much a bar as it is a place to eat, this book aims to be as much a collection of recipes as it is an exploration of the country's drinking culture. The introduction to each recipe describes not just the dish but also the place where I ate it and the people who made it. There is a primer on Thai-style grilling, an essential cooking technique for so much drinking food. You'll also find an exploration of *lao khao*, the original Thai hooch and still the drink of choice for farmers, laborers, and other members of the working class, and of beer, which is closely associated with Thai food in the West but is in fact a modern (and for many, an unaffordable) addition to the bar.

In particular, the book focuses on the drinking culture up-country, in the Northern provinces, where I've traveled the most and which I know the best. What I've left out is either due to my limited knowledge (Southern Thailand is still a relative mystery to me, and I certainly won't claim comprehensive knowledge of the food of the North) or my limited interests: in Bangkok, if you're up for it, you can go to a bar where you can recline on a bed while drinking a cocktail made with dry ice, but my enthusiasms lie elsewhere. It also deserves note that the title of the book is *The Drinking Food of Thailand*, not *Thai Drinking Food*. This might seem like a minor distinction, but it's an important one. It's meant to emphasize that the dishes eaten in Thailand have points of origin as diverse as the peoples and ethnicities—Thai, Tai Yai, Chinese, Burmese, Lao, among others—who make up the population of the country.

For the most part, the recipes in this book will be easier to cook than those in my first book, *Pok Pok: Food and Stories from the Streets, Homes, and Roadside Restaurants of Thailand*. This is not because I've dumbed them down, but rather because drinking food tends to require less work than other culinary categories. A crowd of spent beer bottles is less likely to share the table with sophisticated curries than it is with grilled meats and other simple snacks. Dishes that might include many ingredients when they're made for a housewarming ceremony or dinner party get stripped down to their elements at a shabby tavern. In *Pok Pok*, for example, I provide a recipe from my friend Sunny for a salad of glass noodles that's kitted out with shrimp, ground pork, and fried shallots and garlic. In this book, you'll find the dish's booze-friendly alter ego, a blazing-hot, bracingly sour, garlicky rendition that lacks embellishment.

While you won't find many especially complicated recipes, you'll still find thorough recipes. Don't confuse detail for difficulty. Detail is necessary because my goal is to have you re-create particular dishes with particular flavors, just as they exist in Thailand. Some of the cooking techniques are unfamiliar and thus call for a little extra explanation. Many of the flavors are new, so the recipes require especially precise measurements and more than the typical "season to taste" instruction to get you where you want to be. That said, there is no right way to cook anything, which means that ultimately the particulars of the final product are up to you.

You won't find ingredient substitutions here, unless I've decided that the resulting dish won't suffer from them. The good news is that I don't call for a single ingredient—okay, maybe just two, *makhwen* and *ma laep*—that you can't find in the States, and I provide sources and tips to help you in your search. You'll probably have to visit your local Asian supermarket—that's part of the fun—or at least order from the numerous Thai-focused online grocers.

Luung (uncle) Wut, grill master and chief beef smasher at Paa Daeng Jin Tup.

ABOUT THIS BOOK

First things first: unlike the recipes in many cookbooks on the food of Thailand, those included here are not meant to be eaten as part of a proper meal, that is, several different, communal dishes paired with plenty of rice. It's drinking food, remember, to be snacked on while you make merry. The genre can be tricky to define for two reasons: Thais often drink with dinner, and some dishes in this book, like Naam Phrik Num (Green chile dip), page 71, and Yam Plaa Meuk (Squid salad), page 172, could be considered part of a proper meal were they served with lots of rice. What I've come to understand is that drinking foods are defined as much by what they are as by whether they're eaten with rice, or at least enough to fill you up. In other words, in the first book, rice is essential. Here, it's optional.

All of this is reflected in the serving size in each recipe. Keep that in mind as you cook, so you're not surprised when a dish said to feed four does so as a snack, not as dinner. Remember, too, that the flavors are often intense. You might think you'd prefer to take down a whole bowl of *tom saep*, but that first bite will likely set you straight. Yet like so much drinking food, *tom saep* could serve as dinnertime stuff, rather than as late-night entertainment, along with a bunch of other food. In other words, it's up to you. And some dishes, like *yam* (salads) and certain grilled items, can be doubled or tripled without burden. Others, like stir-fries, can't be, since crowding a wok with twice the amount of each ingredient you're meant to use will yield an unrecognizable product. In cases when making a small portion is unfeasible or when a dish requires an awful amount of work, the recipe I've provided makes a larger portion. That just means you should invite more friends over.

I will not insist on how you serve what you make. But I will say that this kind of food is typically eaten from a communal plate rather than divvied up among individual ones. That goes not only for grilled meats and snacks but also for stir-fries, salads, and soups.

The dishes in this book are divided into rough categories. Consider using these to plan your cooking. *Yam* (salads), by and large, have similar flavor profiles: spicy, tart, funky. Same is true for *tom* (soups), which tend to be sour, spicy, and herbaceous. *Naam phrik* (chile dips) have different flavors and textures but similar purposes. So one dish from each category per evening of revelry will usually suffice. If you're going to prepare a pot of hot oil or a bed of charcoal, however, you might want to prepare a few kinds of fried or grilled items to make it worth the effort.

As for the recipes themselves, each one is meant to guide you to a particular dish that I've eaten in Thailand. Because that dish isn't spaghetti carbonara or Caesar salad, doing it justice requires a little more attention to detail in the kitchen, and rounding up the ingredients calls for a little more effort. You'll even have to buy some special equipment (see page 257).

That said, this food is not hard to cook. It becomes even easier once you get the hang of certain Thai techniques that may not be as familiar as dicing and straining. But they aren't difficult, either, and in some cases, they are actually less onerous than some Western kitchen practices. Your task gets easier still with one big shopping trip to an Asian market with a solid Southeast Asian section. Many items, like bottled sauces and dried ingredients, last indefinitely in your pantry and fridge. Others, like fresh Thai chiles, galangal, and makrut lime leaves, will keep in the freezer for months.

Weight is the preferred measurement for most solid ingredients in this book. It is, simply, more precise. Precision is especially important in a book full of unfamiliar ingredients, techniques, and flavors, where the culinary instincts that might otherwise offset a lack of rigor don't apply. (When the finished product won't suffer, however, I've provided approximate volume equivalents.) So buy an inexpensive digital scale that handles both US units of measurement (ounces and pounds) and metric units (grams and kilograms). You'll like it.

Of course, these recipes, like all recipes, are open to interpretation. There's no right way to make them — not in Thailand and not in your home. Still, I recommend hewing closely to the instructions at first. Until you've cooked a dish my way and experienced the contours of its flavors and textures, make substitutions and omissions at your own peril.

USING A MORTAR AND PESTLE

The mortar is so essential to Thai cooking that I named my restaurant in its honor. *Pok pok* is onomatopoeic for the sound a pestle makes when it strikes the mortar during the making of papaya salad. The mortar is a rudimentary tool that's virtually indispensable in the Thai kitchen. A food processor or a blender is more convenient, but neither one does the job as well as the preindustrial tool.

For many dishes in this book, you'll need a Thai granite mortar and pestle to pound pastes. There is no substitute. Sometimes you'll use them simply to bruise or break up ingredients. The mortar and pestle are my preferred tools for these tasks as well, but you can get away with using the flat surface of a knife blade, the bottom of a pan, or another blunt, heavy object.

Although each recipe provides the information necessary for pounding, the technique deserves a little elaboration. To steady the mortar and reduce the impact of the pounding on the work surface, set the mortar on a folded towel. If you're working on a table, position the mortar over the leg to blunt the impact. Keep your wrist fairly loose as you pound, letting the weight of the pestle do most of the work. However, keep in mind that "pound" means *really* pound, so do some damage. To pound effectively, don't just pummel ingredients from overhead. As you bring the pestle down, aim for the wall of the mortar just above the ingredient and let gravity guide the pestle down the wall toward the bottom. This pestle-sliding-down-wall action creates the friction necessary to break down resistant ingredients.

Pound the ingredients one type at a time, completely pulverizing one ingredient before adding the next, in the order listed in each recipe. In general, you'll start with the toughest, most fibrous ingredients: add each of these ingredients to the center of the mortar, pound firmly to flatten and begin to break them down, and then use the pestle to crush and scrape them against the walls of the mortar to make the paste. As you incorporate softer, wetter ingredients, the paste will become slick, and it'll take more time to incorporate the newcomers. Instead of pounding, focus on scraping and crushing the ingredients against the walls of the mortar.

LAO KHAO

Rice whiskey

เหล้าขาว

In 2010, I attended the Songkhran celebration in the village of Baan Mai in Northern Thailand. I've been going to Baan Mai for more than a decade. My friend Sunny once lived there in a simple home where I watched him make *laap* (minced meat cooked with dried spices) and *khanom* (Thai sweets). Nowadays, I go to visit his sister and buy her *phrik laap*, the seasoning mixture used to make *laap*.

Songkhran is a mid-April festival that marks the Thai New Year. In Baan Mai, the celebration begins at the modest village temple, where residents gather to chant alongside the monks to *tham boon* (pray for good fortune for someone other than yourself) and to symbolically prop up a Bodhi Tree, the type under which Lord Buddha attained enlightenment, in a gesture of support for Buddhism itself.

Soon, worship becomes revelry. A stage appears in front of the temple. Food vendors, hired for the day, set up shop. While a soundtrack of extremely loud music blares from mammoth speakers in the bed of a pickup, everyone gets frequently and summarily splashed with water. The tradition represents washing away the bad of the previous year and conveniently coincides with the hottest month. Soaked to their skin, people of the village eat and drink. Oh brother, do they drink—and not just men (historically, imbibing was primarily a masculine exercise). The whole town is hammered.

If a person runs up to you and doesn't splash you with water, he or she is offering you a drink, most often *lao khao*. Roughly translated as "rice whiskey," it's the liquor of choice for working-class Thais, particularly in the sticky rice country of the North and Northeast. Understanding *lao khao* is a crucial part of understanding the *aahaan kap klaem* (drinking food) featured in this book. Most of these dishes come from the Northern countryside, where *lao khao* likely animated the cooks who dreamed them up and therefore helps explain why the food is the way it is.

Made from fermented sticky rice, *lao khao* can be cruel. Most renditions employ commercial yeast and have a flavor that is marginally more delicious than gasoline. However, if you're making three hundred baht (about nine dollars) a day toiling for twelve hours in the rice fields, you come home not only eager for a drink but also eager for that drink to be strong and cheap. Two bottles of *lao khao* cost about 130 baht and will get two guys drunk. Two similar-size bottles of beer cost about the same and will get no guys drunk.

Until about the mid-2000s, making *lao khao* in Thailand was illegal. When Sunny was a boy, villagers made it on outdoor stoves only for special occasions like Songkhran. Before the government began inspecting facilities and taxing sales, enterprising Thai moonshiners operated small stills in the jungle or forest to evade detection. They built their stills near rivers, using water and gravity to provide the flow of coolant essential for distillation.

Today, in contrast, it's part of the local economy. Just as Sunny's sister makes and sells *phrik laap*, two distilleries produce the *lao khao* sold to general stores and markets near Baan Mai. Both are located in the village and are separated by a five-minute walk. One is an unsanctioned spin-off of the other. Whatever rivalry exists between the two operations proceeds without incident. Although the days of the entire village joining forces to plant, harvest, and thresh rice are long gone, a communal spirit still thrives. Everyone is either related to or knows one another. There are few fences separating properties. You can walk from yard to yard all the way from the bodega on the main road to the rice fields. When I go to Baan Mai with Sunny, he'll enter someone's yard, yell a name, and inform the owner that he's taking some fruit from her tree.

For years I've been visiting the original distillery in Baan Mai. Only recently did I pry details from Win, the guy who runs it. This is how it goes in Thailand, where people tend to respond to my interest in their process with confusion or even slight irritation. Sometimes I feel as if I'm asking a construction worker about the intricacies of his jackhammering. Making whiskey is not Win's art. It's his job. His goal is to produce *lao khao* with efficiency and profitability. Demand is not a problem. Besides his standard distribution, orders pour in for occasions that prompt particularly heavy consumption—weddings, funerals, housewarmings. He told me that the people in the village "have to" drink—not want to, *have to*. His pronouncement encompasses people like himself, who work hard and require nightly escape, and people like his uncle, a toothless elderly man who lives here too and "takes no vacation" from drinking, day or night.

A stout man of forty who wears a uniform of flip-flops, basketball shorts, and a T-shirt, Win operates the stills almost every day. He takes off only on Buddhist holidays, days that are considered unlucky, and on those rare occasions when his supply exceeds orders. He is at least the third generation to make this particular *lao khao* (or *lao klan*, a sort of branding effort meaning "drip whiskey" that sounds a bit cooler). When Win was a young kid, his father acquired the recipe for the yeast from his own father, who had acquired it from someone else. Eight years ago, Win quit his job in a factory to help his father make *lao khao*. He has no kids yet, but when he stops working here, I have no doubt someone will take over—a cousin, an uncle, a friend. The business makes money, after all.

Yet don't be fooled. Win may not fetishize his product or seem particularly proud of his methods, but he doesn't just dump rice into a bucket to ferment, either. His family performs the process the way a career line cook grills a steak—not lovingly but expertly. Quality means customers. Their *lao khao* is the best I've had.

Of particular importance is the yeast recipe his grandfather acquired long ago. Today, Win's father still adds to the starter a mixture of aromatics like lemongrass, galangal, and chiles, which come through in the finished product. On my last visit, Win underscored their significance when he showed me a bottle of *shochu*, the Japanese distilled spirit made from barley, rice, or sweet potato, that a friend had brought him from a trip to Japan. It's safe to say that most *shochu* is made in a more modern facility with more refined methods than those used to make *lao khao*. Still, Win politely expressed his disapproval for the foreign product in a typically Thai way: "*Mai hom*" (There's no aroma), he said. In Thailand, aroma is almost as important as flavor. This applies to booze as well as food. And like appreciating the food of Thailand, appreciating the booze begins with understanding the process employed to make it. So here goes nothing.

THE PROCESS

1 Every three or so days, Win's father and aunt fabricate yeast cakes. They make a paste with water; ground sticky rice (from their own fields); pounded garlic, fresh chiles, lemongrass, and galangal (all of which grow profusely nearby); and a Chinese mixture of dried spices. Seated beside a pickup truck in an open-air garage near their home, they mold this paste into rough disks (about five inches in diameter and an inch thick), pressing each one with a finger to create an indentation that makes them easier to pick up later.

2 As they form the disks, they lay them onto a bed of rice hay. They sprinkle the tops of the disks with pulverized yeast cakes from the previous batch (what these disks will soon become) and then spray them with some *lao khao*.

3 Next, they cover the disks with a bamboo latticework, top it with a layer of rice hay, and finally with heavy blankets. This creates a hot environment that's ideal for yeast propagation. The ambient micro-organisms, as well as the aromatics, the disks absorb determine the particular character of Win's *lao khao*—what you might call its *terroir*.

4 After about two days, they unveil the swollen disks and set them on a chicken-wire drying rack in the sun until they're fully dry. This takes anywhere from three to five days, depending on the weather. If orders for *lao khao* are particularly heavy, they might expedite the drying by crumbling the yeast cakes after a day or two.

5 Crushed and then passed through a grinder, the yeast joins a large quantity of steamed sticky rice and water in plastic buckets. In the old days, these containers would have been made of clay. Stacks of buckets—in many stages of fermentation—nearly fill the scruffy shed beside the stills, pervading the air with a sour scent. There is no temperature control here, as there might be in a factory; only the predictably scalding weather.

6 Win monitors the progress as the rice ferments for five to eight days and gives off an amber liquid. A good look and sniff tell him when each bucket is ready. He strains out the rice and keeps the liquid. This liquid (*sah to*) is what people drank in the days before distillation and occasionally even today. There's often a plastic water bottle full of it in the fridge of the village bodega.

7 Win operates two stills: three-foot-high oil drums set above roaring wood fires. The wood, tens of thousands of baht worth every year, comes from *longan*, *lam yai*, and other trees that no longer produce fruit. It burns hot and long. Propane has advantages over wood. If Win were to use it, he wouldn't have to get up at dawn to start the fire. Nor would he have to monitor the fire constantly to prevent it from becoming too hot, which can turn the distilled spirit cloudy. But propane is expensive and would cut into his profits. Plus, the *lao khao* wouldn't taste quite the same without some of that smoke flavor creeping in.

Win pours the fermented rice liquid into the drums, sets a large wok on top of each drum, wraps rotten (and therefore supple) banana stems around the sides of each wok to create a seal, and fills the wok with cool water. Even though his process (known as *tom lao*, or "to boil liquor") is low-tech, his goal is the same as that of most distillers. He will bring the slightly alcoholic liquid to a temperature below 212°F / 100°C, at which pure water boils, and above 173°F / 78°C, at which pure alcohol boils. The alcohol-rich vapor he creates rises, hits the bottom of the relatively cool wok, and condenses from vapor back into liquid. The liquid drips down into a catch pan attached to a pipe built into the side of the drum, trickling out of the pipe into a funnel set in an awaiting gas can.

To maintain the temperature and ensure condensation, Win frequently feeds the fire and occasionally pours more cool water into the wok. After two to three hours, the container fills with three to four gallons of liquid that is about 80 percent alcohol. This liquid is called *hua*, or "the head." He continues the process, replacing the gas can, to capture a weaker brew of about 5 percent alcohol, which is known as *hang*, or "the tail." The terms *hua* and *hang* are also used to describe the process of making coconut cream (the head) and coconut milk (the tail). As long as there's still liquid in the oil drum, Win can boil it to create more and more tail. But the tail is weak stuff, and at some point, he calls it quits.

8 Next, Win mixes together the head and tail to achieve a mixture that's sixty proof, then passes the liquid through a rustic filter of polyester batting impregnated with charcoal.

9 His aunt, seated on a low stool, pours the filtered spirit through a funnel into bottles. She gets drunk every time from the fumes, she says, offering no sign that she's joking. A green-and-yellow label that shows two clasped hands is then stuck on each bottle. Their product is Tra Meu, or "Hand Brand."

10 The bottle caps go on, the government stickers (which cost them about fifty thousand baht each month) are affixed to the caps, and the bottles are sent off to market. Then the process begins all over again.

KHAWNG WAANG

SNACKS

ของว่าง

KAI SAAM YANG

ไก่สามอย่าง   Chicken three ways

The first thing you need to know about *kai saam yang*, or "chicken three ways," is that the snack does not contain chicken—or any meat, for that matter. The name reportedly came about during a time when chicken was scarce, when you ate what you had and cracked jokes to endure the lot life brought. The second thing you need to know is that while the English translation makes it sound like an overwrought creation served at some Michelin-starred restaurant, the dish itself is utterly rudimentary: a collection of raw ingredients chopped or sliced, piled on a plate, and eaten with a spoon—one intense bite at a time. Basic though it is, the flavors are evocatively Thai and represent drinking food at its finest.

I've eaten many versions in Thailand, from the extremely simple (just peanuts, lemongrass, and shallots) to the merely very simple (additions of Thai chiles, ginger, and peel-on pinkie-tip-size garlic cloves). I've heard of versions made with crunchy fried bugs, no great stretch in Thailand and a reasonable source of protein when poultry is unavailable. The recipe here is for my preferred combination, which you'll discover makes a compulsively delicious snack with any booze, whether you mix all of the ingredients together, eat each separately, or something in between.

◊ ◊ ◊

An extra-fancy rendition of *kai saam yang* with dried shrimp.

2 Key limes, or 1 regular (Persian) lime

17 g / 2 tablespoons diced (¼ inch / 6 mm) peeled Asian shallots

16 g / 2 tablespoons diced (¼ inch / 6 mm) peeled fresh ginger

12 g / 2 tablespoons sliced (¼ inch / 6 mm) fresh Thai chiles, preferably red

14 g / 2 tablespoons thinly sliced (⅛ inch / 3 mm) lemongrass (tender parts only)

40 g / ¼ cup salted roasted Spanish (red-skinned) peanuts

14 g / 2 tablespoons Kung Haeng Khua (Dry-fried dried shrimp), page 239

Executing this recipe is a no-brainer. Still, you can up your game by choosing small hands of thin-skinned ginger and smooth, glossy-skinned limes. The former tend to be less fibrous, and the latter tend to have less pith and more juice than their dull, rough-peel counterparts. That's all the better, of course, since you're eating both of them raw, and in the case of the lime, with the peel and pith intact.

◊ *serves 2 to 4*

Wash the limes especially well, since you'll be eating the peel as well as the flesh. Cut off both ends of each lime to reveal the flesh, and stand a lime on one of the flat ends. Cutting from the top to the bottom and following the contour of the fruit, cut off pieces ¼ inch / 6 mm thick that include both the peel and the flesh, then cut the pieces into ¼-inch / 6-mm dice. Repeat with the second lime. You'll need 20 g / 2 tablespoons diced lime for this recipe. Reserve the remainder for another use.

Arrange the lime, shallots, ginger, chiles, lemongrass, peanuts, and shrimp each in its own pile on a small plate. Serve with spoons.

PLAA LEK THAWT KROB

Fried tiny fish   ปลาเล็กทอดกรอบ

In the same way you might grab chips on your way to a friend's house in the States, you might grab a couple of small plastic bags of these deep-fried dried anchovies at a roadside stand or convenience store in Thailand. Someone might break out a bottle of sauce *phrik*, a sweet, ketchuplike chile sauce, and blammo, you've got a killer snack to have with drinks. To my taste, a Thai-made Sriracha, such as Shark brand—not the ubiquitous Vietnamese-American Huy Fong (rooster) brand, which is a totally different product—makes a good thing even better. ◊ *serves 4 to 6*

Note on Dried Anchovies: Most Asian markets in the States have a dizzying array of dried fish in bags and bins, with the English labeling ranging from vague to nonexistent. To find the dried anchovies you need for this recipe, look for the word *anchovies*, though your best bet is to go by appearance, choosing thin, silvery dried fish 1 to 2 inches / 2.5 to 5 cm long. If you have a choice, a higher price generally indicates better quality, or at least guides you toward unbroken fish. You'll find dried anchovies at most good Asian markets, though I've found that Korean markets often have the best selection.

◊ ◊ ◊

Line a large sheet pan with paper towels or newspaper. Rinse the anchovies under lukewarm water, drain well, and spread them out in a single layer on the towel-lined pan. Pat the fish gently with more paper towels and let them sit at room temperature until fully dry, about 3 hours.

Select a heavy pot at least 12 inches / 30 cm wide and pour in the oil to a depth of 2 to 3 inches / 5 to 7.5 cm. Set the pot over high heat and heat the oil to 325°F / 165°C. Use the thermometer to test the temperature, measuring the oil at the center of the vessel and carefully stirring the oil occasionally to ensure a consistent temperature.

Line the large pan with fresh paper towels or newspaper. When the anchovies are dry, carefully add them all at once to the hot oil and fry, stirring occasionally, until they are crispy and turn a shade or two darker, about 2 minutes. Using the spider or a mesh strainer, transfer them to the prepared pan.

Serve right away with the sauce for dipping.

SPECIAL EQUIPMENT

A deep-fry thermometer

A large spider skimmer (recommended)

---

1 (6-ounce / 170-g) package tiny dried anchovies (see Note, page 23)

Neutral oil (such as soybean or palm), for deep-frying (about 12 cups / 2.8 L)

Shark brand Sriracha or sweet Thai chile sauce

THUA THAWT SAMUN PHRAI

ถั่วทอดสมุนไพร **Fried peanuts with makrut lime leaves, garlic, and chiles**

SPECIAL EQUIPMENT

A deep-fry thermometer

A large spider skimmer (recommended)

Neutral oil (such as soybean or palm), for deep-frying (about 2 cups / 480 ml)

36 g / 3 tablespoons finely chopped (⅛ inch / 3 mm) garlic

2 g / about 5 dried Thai chiles

5 g / 6 large fresh or thawed frozen makrut lime leaves, patted dry

455 g / 3 cups unsalted Spanish (red-skinned) peanuts

4 g / 1¼ teaspoons kosher salt

When I first started traveling to Thailand, peanuts like these often came complimentary with your beer at drinking establishments, particularly those that served *farang* like myself. Nowadays you see them everywhere—markets, bus stops, bars—though they're rarely free. You'll even see a sort of kitchen-sink version, *thua raboert* (explosion peanuts), that includes ingredients like dried shrimp, dried anchovies, lemongrass, and cashews. So go wild. But first make this version. What makes it great is the dried chiles, makrut lime leaves, and garlic, all fried to a fragrant crisp, that infuse salty peanuts with flavor.

◊ *serves 8 to 10*

Line a large sheet pan with paper towels or newspaper. Set a fine-mesh strainer over a heatproof container. Pour the oil to a depth of ¾ inch / 2 cm or so into a wok or large saucepan and set the wok over high heat until the oil is 275°F / 135°C. Use the thermometer to test the temperature, measuring the oil at the center of the vessel and carefully stirring the oil occasionally to ensure a consistent temperature.

Add all of the garlic to the hot oil, immediately turn down the heat to low, and stir the garlic. Cook, stirring occasionally and adjusting the heat to maintain a gentle sizzle, until the garlic is light golden brown and

◊ ◊ ◊

completely crisp, 4 to 6 minutes. Pour the contents of the wok through the prepared strainer. Transfer the garlic to a corner of the prepared pan.

Return the oil to the wok and set over medium-low heat. Add the chiles and cook, stirring often, until they turn a deep, dark brown (but not black), 5 to 8 minutes. Using the spider or a mesh strainer, transfer the chiles to the prepared pan to drain. Scoop out any loose seeds from the oil.

Increase the heat to high and bring the oil to 300°F / 150°C. Add the lime leaves and cook, stirring occasionally, until the leaves are crisp but still bright green, about 10 seconds. Using the spider, transfer them to the prepared pan to drain. Lower the heat to medium.

Once again, set the fine-mesh strainer over the heatproof container. Add the peanuts to the hot oil and cook, stirring constantly, until light golden brown, 7 to 8 minutes. Pour the contents of the wok through the prepared strainer and transfer the peanuts to an empty part of the prepared pan. Reserve the oil for another use.

When the peanuts are cool enough to handle but still warm, transfer them to a large bowl. Add the garlic, chiles, lime leaves, and salt and, using your hands, mix well, crushing the chiles and lime leaves so they break into small pieces. Taste and adjust the seasoning with salt.

Serve warm or at room temperature. The mixture will keep in an airtight container in a cool, dark place for up to 2 weeks.

KUNG TEN

Dancing shrimp   กุ้งเต้น

Two decades ago, i was passing an afternoon in one of the thatch-roofed huts that line the bank of Huay Teung Thao. A reservoir on the road from Chiang Mai to the quiet town of Mae Rim, it serves as a site for family fun—swimming, frollicking, and because this is Thailand, eating. In fact, it's a rare thing to see a picturesque body of water around these parts without some operation selling food on the premises.

    The little kitchen my friends and I chose for lunch was known for *kung ten* (dancing shrimp), one of those dishes that make skittish Westerners squirm and give intrepid backpackers a good story to tell back at the hostel. When we ordered, a woman sauntered to a pen submerged in the reservoir—within a few feet, it must be noted, from thrashing children—and used a small net to scoop out a few dozen tiny live shrimp. She deposited the shrimp in an earthenware bowl, while another cook made the dressing, poured it on top of the shrimp, and quickly covered them with an inverted glass bowl. We watched as the shrimp did what you'd probably do if someone doused you with a vat of lime juice and chiles—they went bonkers. Once they stopped dancing, it was time to eat.

    Part of the dish's appeal is the novelty of seeing the shrimp flail and jerk—dancing, of course, is just one way to describe what they're doing—all the while underscoring the freshness of the seafood. After all, what's fresher than creatures that were alive seconds before you ate them? When the novelty wears off, you're left with the familiar thrill of Thai *yam*—the fierce heat of fresh chiles, the bracing tartness from lime, the saltiness and umami from fish sauce. (Since that first encounter, I've also eaten *kung ten* prepared with the

◊ ◊ ◊

A Thai granite mortar
and pestle

A small, clear glass bowl,
if using live shrimp

———

1½ tablespoons fresh lime
juice, preferably from
Key limes or from regular
(Persian) limes spiked with
a small squeeze of Meyer
lemon juice

1½ tablespoons Thai fish
sauce

4 g / 1 teaspoon
granulated sugar

14 g / 4 peeled garlic cloves,
halved lengthwise

6 g / 4 stemmed fresh Thai
chiles, preferably green

16 g / 2 tablespoons thinly
sliced (with the grain)
peeled Asian shallots

14 g / 2 tablespoons thinly
sliced lemongrass (tender
parts only), from about
2 large stalks

4 g / 2 tablespoons
coarsely chopped cilantro
(thin stems and leaves)

5 g / 1 tablespoon sliced
(¼ inch / 6 mm) green
onions

2 ounces / 55 g very small
raw shrimp (see Note),
preferably whole and alive
(⅓ cup)

Pinch of kosher salt

flavors of Isaan *laap*, including dried-chile powder and toasted-rice powder.)

The intrepid among you will seek out tiny live shrimp sold in tanks for well-stocked Asian markets. But if you must settle for top-quality, recently killed crustaceans, then you'll still be able to make something worth eating. Though there won't be any dancing, that's for sure.

◊ *serves 8 to 10*

Note on Live Shrimp: Some Asian markets sell the live, tiny shrimp that *kung ten* requires. Without live crustaceans, your shrimp certainly won't dance, of course. Yet as long as they're very fresh, you can make a reasonable approximation of this dish. Look for either frozen raw shrimp the size of bay shrimp in the freezer case or buy good-looking raw shrimp, peel them, and cut them into small pieces to approximate the size of the tiny ones.

Combine the lime juice, fish sauce, and sugar in a small serving bowl and stir to dissolve the sugar.

Pound the garlic and chiles in the mortar to a very coarse paste, about 15 seconds. Transfer 12 g / 1 tablespoon of the mixture or more to taste to the bowl and add the shallots, lemongrass, cilantro, and green onions.

If you're using live shrimp, add the shrimp to the serving bowl, sprinkle on the salt, and invert the clear glass bowl over the serving bowl. At the table, shake well and watch the show. When the party's over, remove the glass bowl and serve.

If you're not using live shrimp, add the shrimp to the serving bowl, sprinkle on the salt, stir well, and serve.

◊ ◊ ◊

A shrimp makes a final, futile break for it.

PLAA MEUK PING

ปลาหมึกปิ้ง   **Grilled dried cuttlefish**

You're sitting outdoors at a roadside pub in Thailand at a table cluttered with glasses of beer and plates of food when he pulls up on a bike-powered cart, announcing his arrival with a few honks of a horn. Attached to the cart is a tempting display: rows of dried cuttlefish clothespinned to a rack.

The conduct of the *plaa meuk ping* hawker runs contrary to Western business etiquette. He makes rounds of all of the drinking establishments in town, even those that serve food, but no one chases him away. Instead, people queue up, pointing to the best-looking specimen on his rack. They mill about as the vendor briefly toasts the dried cuttlefish over charcoal, then runs it through what looks like a hand-crank pasta maker or sugarcane crusher, depending on your frame of reference. Grilling adds a smoky fragrance, and a back-and-forth trip through the contraption flattens and tenderizes the cuttlefish and marks it with grooves, so you can tear it by hand into bite-size strands.

Like most Americans who have happily killed an hour in an Asian market, I have bought plastic bags of dried shredded cuttlefish. But this commercially manufactured iteration is an entirely different experience from the freshly grilled version—warm, full of deep umami, and when cooked correctly, counterintuitively juicy to the bite. Dipped in a bit of sweet chile sauce, the salty, chewy strands are hard to resist, even when your table is always crowded with plates.

I don't provide a proper recipe for this dish because it requires that hand-crank machine, which you don't have and are highly unlikely to purchase. But for the curious reader (or the truly ambitious cook), I buy BDMP—good old Bangkok Dehydrated Marine Product—brand dried cuttlefish, and bigger creatures at that, with hoods that measure 4 to 6 inches / 10 to 15 cm across. I separate the tentacles from the hood and grill both parts over a relatively low charcoal fire, flipping the pieces occasionally, just until they begin to curl a bit and are toasty and slightly puffed. The tentacles take a bit longer than the hoods.

I insert each cuttlefish hood into the rollers of the machine (the tentacles don't need rolling out), which I bought in Thailand before I knew I could get more or less the same one at Lax-C, also known as Thai Costco, in LA. I turn the crank back and forth quickly, running the entire length of the hood through the ridged rollers several times. Then I serve the hoods and the tentacles with Naam Jim Kai (Sweet chile dipping sauce), page 244, for dipping.

PHRIK KLEUA

Salt-chile dip for green mango   พริกเกลือ

Even the most informal bars in Thailand have food. By day, a table on the sidewalk might host a modest pork butcher shop. By night, a relative of the pork butcher runs a curbside drinking establishment, with the same table now draped with an oilcloth. There's an ice bucket, a pitcher of water, and assorted bottles of rice-based liquor, like *lao khao*, *ya dawng*, and Sang Som, the ubiquitous brand of Thai rum. A woman dispenses shots to men who have already consumed enough to tell you loudly in English that you will "save the world." You slowly realize that they're referring to the movie *Armageddon*. This is not the first time a drunk Thai man has informed you that you look like Bruce Willis.

At a place like this, the food on offer is simple—probably sliced fresh fruit with salty-sweet chile powder for dipping. I especially like it when the fruit is green mango, which is crunchy and far more tart than sweet. In the States, there's pretty much just one variety to choose from. Sold mainly at Southeast Asian and South Asian markets, the green mangoes you're after aren't just firm and unripe but also actually green—not mottled or greenish—in color. ◊ *serves 4 to 8*

SPECIAL EQUIPMENT
A Thai granite mortar and pestle

---

4 g / 12 stemmed dried Thai chiles

100 g / ½ cup rock sugar

36 g / ¼ cup kosher salt

2 green mangoes, peeled, pitted, and cut into spears

Firmly pound the chiles in the mortar to a fairly fine powder. Add the sugar and pound to a fairly fine powder. Add the salt, mix, then pound until the mixture has the texture of granulated sugar. You should have about 85 g / ½ cup. It will keep in an airtight container in a cool, dark place for up to 2 weeks.

Serve the mangoes with about 22 g / 2 tablespoons of the chile mixture.

YAM MET MAMUANG HIMAPHAAN

Fried cashews with salt, chiles, and green onions

ยำเม็ดมะม่วงหิมพานต์

Bangkok's Lam Sing Pla Tong is part bar, part music hall, and part cabaret. It's on a busy strip that comprises a sort of entertainment district for people from Isaan (Northeast Thailand), who make up a good portion of the working class in the city. All of the city's cab drivers, primarily men from Isaan, seem to know the place. The crowd is a mix of construction workers, also primarily men from Isaan; women; and *kathoey,* men who dress flamboyantly like women.

Before you pass through the dark door, a gentleman brusquely pats you down to make sure you're not packing. Sadly, in this atmosphere, acts of passion-fueled violence are not uncommon. You join the rabble in the audience, dodging inebriates and noting the visiting dignitaries—and I don't mean heads of state. Amid the shit show, they're the ones with the cherry tables, expensive whiskey, and many admirers who crowd around hoping for handshakes. On a stage that looks as if it's been plastered with glitter, a band plays almost nonstop, and a varying cast of characters—nearly a dozen different singers who later reappear as backup dancers and, sometimes, end up pouring your drinks— perform deafening renditions of songs that everyone

◊ ◊ ◊

A deep-fry thermometer

A large spider skimmer (recommended)

———

Neutral oil (such as soybean or palm) for deep-frying (about ½ cup / 120 ml)

85 g / ½ cup raw cashews

1 g / ½ teaspoon kosher salt

10 g / 2 tablespoons sliced (¼ inch / 6 mm) green onions

6 g / 1 tablespoon sliced (¼ inch / 6 mm) fresh Thai chiles, preferably red

but you seems to know. The music is *morlam* and *lukthung,* mournful songs depicting the hardships of country living or ribald stories of love. The numbers are highly choreographed. Some particularly happy customers show their appreciation by stuffing money into shirt collars and waistbands.

A couple of friends, two longtime expats and enthusiastic explorers, put me onto this place, which they stumbled into while on the prowl for duck *laap.* As soon as I got to Bangkok—or at least, after a few plates of *laap* and some deep-fried duck bills at a restaurant next door—I went to experience Lam Sing Pla Tong for myself. The night before I flew back to the States, I went again. I came for the fun. I came back for the cashews.

To sustain us that first night, my entourage and I ordered a few dishes from the menu, a typical booze-friendly collection of fried stuff and salads but with an Isaan bent. What got me was a plate of fried cashews, aggressively salted and tossed with roughly chopped green onions and fresh red chiles in chunks big enough to inspire alarm. I spent the rest of the night shoveling down this salty, spicy, crunchy snack between slugs of beer.

Since then, I've ordered the dish every time I've spotted it. Sometimes what I receive is a variation that's closer to *yam* (or so-called Thai salads), complete with fish sauce, lime juice, raw shallots, and ground pork. The version at Lam Sing Pla Tong reflects the dish at its simplest. And it's the one I like best. ◊ *serves 2 to 4*

Pour the oil to a depth of ½ inch / 12 mm into small saucepan, set over medium heat, and heat to 325°F / 165°C. Use the thermometer to test the temperature, measuring the oil at the center of the vessel and carefully stirring the oil occasionally to ensure a consistent temperature. Line a bowl with paper towels or newspaper and put it near the stove.

Carefully add the cashews to the hot oil and cook, stirring constantly, until light golden brown, 1 to 2 minutes. Keep in mind that the cashews will get a shade or two darker once they leave the oil. Using the spider or a slotted spoon, transfer the cashews to the prepared bowl to drain. Immediately season the cashews with the salt, tossing them as you season.

Transfer the nuts to a plate and sprinkle on the green onions and chiles. Serve warm.

YA DAWNG

ยาดอง   **Herbal rice whiskey**

If you haven't been to Thailand, chances are you haven't had *ya dawng*. Come to think of it, even if you have been to Thailand, chances are you haven't had *ya dawng*.

Farang don't typically venture to the places that serve the drink. *Ya dawng* is essentially *lao khao* (distilled rice alcohol) that has been infused with different combinations of herbs and roots with various curative properties—with a clear focus, as has been not so subtly suggested to me many times, on increased virility. In general, Thais tend to take the opposite view of alcohol's effect on a particular sort of performance than folks do in the West.

The drink has long had a reputation as crude country stuff. But despite a recent government crackdown on stalls that sell liquor made with black-market *lao khao*, there are some glimmers of a resurgence, including a few spiffy-looking bars in Bangkok that mix cocktails with house-made *ya dawng*.

I still don't fully understand this particular genre of Thai booze and its connections to folk medicine. I do, however, enjoy parking myself at the nighttime carts, stalls, and other less formal operations—a wood plank balanced on crates, a simple stand that by day housed a food vendor— that dispense *ya dawng*. In my experience, the customers will almost always be, for better or worse, men, and the atmosphere will be one of heavy drinking and shit talking.

Even though there's no kitchen, there's almost always food. A plate or two will likely be set out with fruit for the taking—pods of sour tamarind, the intensely tart and tannic *mayom* (star gooseberry), or sliced unripe mango.

As with any product, the quality varies widely. Some spots sell thoughtfully infused stuff made from time-tested recipes, while others just mark up store-bought stuff or buy herbal mixtures that they infuse into *lao khao*. From a medicinal standpoint, it's the difference between going to an herbalist and buying the jar of Horny Goat Weed sold at what seems like every New York City bodega. From a getting-drunk standpoint, it's pretty much the same.

TOM
SOUP

KAENG AWM NEUA

Northern Thai stewed beef   แกงอ่อม

Laap Kao Cham Chaa is what passes for a proper restaurant in Chiang Mai, the laid-back cultural capital of Northern Thailand. *Cham chaa* means "rain tree" and refers to the one around whose trunk the place appears precariously built. People fill small stools crowded at wooden tables. The décor consists of a few filthy, once-colorful ice chests, a three-foot propane tank, and a handful of beat-up lanterns that hang from the aluminum awning, glowing as the day's light fades on Ratanakosin Road.

But don't be fooled by the modest setting. The food here is killer. And business is booming. The boss of the place sits beside a computer screen—a strange sight at a restaurant with no walls—displaying black-and-white security video of the place from various angles. He presides behind a long table draped with black oilcloth and in front of a row of stools. Throughout the night, he totals up checks, poking at a calculator, and riffles through stacks of cash. He also doubles as bartender, pouring slugs of Sang Som or delivering beers to the guys across the table, because while some customers here are enjoying full-on meals, many are here only to drink.

Next to each table is a smaller one holding a bucket of ice and bottles of soda water. Motley groups pour tall boys of Leo beer into glasses. One party has brought a bottle of Johnnie Walker Black Label, a serious splurge in Thailand, where imported whiskey is wildly expensive. They'll probably be here all night, or at least until the bottle's empty.

◊ ◊ ◊

_____

Paste

18 g thinly sliced
lemongrass (tender
parts only), from
about 3 large stalks

8 g kosher salt

25 g peeled fresh or
thawed frozen galangal,
thinly sliced against the
grain

10 g peeled fresh or
thawed frozen yellow
turmeric root, thinly
sliced against the grain

23 g stemmed dried
Mexican puya chiles,
soaked in hot tap water
until fully soft, about
15 minutes

75 g peeled garlic cloves,
halved lengthwise

75 g peeled Asian shallots,
thinly sliced against
the grain

38 g Kapi Kung
(Homemade shrimp paste),
page 238

Yet whether the occasion is dinner or revelry, there's food. It starts coming seconds after you order and keeps on coming as it's ready. Not surprising for a place with the word *laap* in the name, *laap,* minced meat cooked with a paste of dried spices and shrimp paste, is among the plates. So, too, are slowly grilled pork neck and intestines, plucked from glistening piles on a charcoal grill out front and served with fiery tamarind-spiked sauce for dipping. But my spoon is focused on *Kaeng awm neua.*

In Thai, the word *kaeng* refers to what we call curry or soup, or as with *Kaeng awm neua,* something in between. Whatever you call it, the dish doesn't look like much, just small hunks of meat wading in ruddy brown liquid flecked with herbs. Yet it's just as deserving of your attention as anything else on the table. Like many curries, it relies on a paste pounded in a mortar; in this case, one that features a very Northern Thai combination of moderately spicy dried chiles, turmeric root, lemongrass, and galangal. Like many soups, it is brothy, and depending on where you get it and how long it's been sitting on the stove that night, it ranges from stock-thin to stew-thick. Either way, it's salty, spicy, and herbaceous, with each bite satisfyingly intense. The pieces of pork or beef don't collapse with a tap from your spoon like an Italian braise. Instead, the meat has some chew, and the dish is better for it. ◊ *serves 6 to 8*

Make the Paste

Combine the lemongrass and salt in the mortar and pound until you have a fairly smooth, slightly fibrous paste, about 2 minutes. Add the galangal and pound, occasionally stopping to scrape down the sides of the mortar, until you have a fairly smooth paste, about 2 minutes. Do the same with the turmeric.

Drain the chiles well, slit them open, and remove the seeds. Wrap the chiles in paper towels and gently squeeze them dry. Add them to the mortar and pound them, then the garlic, and then the shallots, fully pounding each ingredient before moving on to the next. Finally, add the shrimp paste and pound until it is fully incorporated, about 1 minute.

You'll have about 265 g / 1 cup of paste. You can use it right away, or you can store it in an airtight container in the fridge for up to 1 week or in the freezer for up to 6 months.

Make the soup

Halve the beef shank lengthwise, then cut it against the grain into slices 2 by 1 by ½ inch / 5 by 2.5 cm by 12 mm. Set aside.

Heat the oil in a heavy pot over medium-low heat until it shimmers. Add 265 g / 1 cup of the paste and stir well. Take a careful sniff. You'll smell the raw shallots and garlic. Cook, stirring frequently, until the garlic and shallots no longer smell raw, about 10 minutes. Knowing when it's done takes experience, but as long as you're cooking it at a low sizzle, the soup will taste great.

Raise the heat to medium-high, add the beef, fish sauce, and salt, and stir well to coat the beef with the paste. Cook, stirring frequently, for 10 minutes so the meat absorbs some of the flavors but does not brown.

Add the water, raise the heat to high, and bring to a boil. Meanwhile, lightly smash the lemongrass with a pestle, a pan, or the flat surface of a knife blade, then cut crosswise on the diagonal into 1-inch / 2.5-cm lengths. Reserve 45 g / ½ cup of the lemongrass for this recipe, reserving the rest for another purpose.

When the liquid comes to a boil, lower the heat to medium and add the lemongrass, galangal, and cilantro roots. Tear the lime leaves and add them, too. Cover and cook, adjusting the heat to maintain a gentle simmer, until the beef is tender but still has bite, about 1 hour.

Let the soup cool slightly, then taste and adjust the seasoning with fish sauce. Sprinkle on the cilantro, sawtooth herb, and green onions, and serve right away.

Soup

1 pound, 10 ounces / 750 g boneless beef shank (not trimmed)

1 tablespoon neutral oil (such as rice bran or canola)

2 tablespoons Thai fish sauce

12 g / 1 tablespoon plus 1 teaspoon kosher salt

6½ cups / 1.5 L water

2 stalks lemongrass (about 4 ounces / 115 g total), bottom 1 inch / 2.5 cm, top 9 inches / 23 cm, and outer layer removed

35 g / ¼ cup thinly sliced (⅛ inch / 3 mm) peeled fresh or thawed frozen galangal

12 g / 12 cilantro roots

3 g / 4 large fresh or frozen makrut lime leaves

2 g / 1 tablespoon coarsely chopped cilantro (thin stems and leaves)

2 g / 1 tablespoon thinly sliced sawtooth herb

5 g / 1 tablespoon sliced (¼ inch / 6 mm) green onions

YAM KOP

Northern Thai frog soup   ยำกบ

When I got to the roadside pub on the outskirts of Chiang Mai, there was no menu, and even if there had been, I wouldn't have been able to read it. Good thing I was with my friend and trusty food guru Sunny. I asked him what was on offer, and he rattled off the options: various grilled pig parts, a broth spiked with bitter beef bile, and frog soup. What caught my ear that day was the last. So Sunny put in the order for *yam kop*.

Frog ends up often on the Thai table—I've even snacked on its fried skin, removed more or less intact so the result looks like a creature frozen midswim—and the reason is no mystery. Pigs and chickens take time and money to raise, while frogs ("*kop kop*," they say, as they loiter in ponds and rice paddies) take just your wits and maybe a forked spear to catch. In the North, they often end up in the sort of rustic soup that appeared on our table, one flavored with a coarse paste of chiles, dried spices, and purposefully rotten seafood, as well as fibrous planks of galangal and slices of lemongrass that you dodge with your spoon.

I loved the flavor—hot, salty, funky. I loved the complexity and fragrance from the combination of spices, aromatics, and a last-minute dose of fresh herbs. But I didn't love eating the amphibian itself, the entire creature hacked up into bony, dank-tasting bits. When I learned to make the dish, I conceded one aspect to my Western tastes: instead of whole frogs, I use only the dainty legs. But don't let me stop you from experiencing the real deal. Most Asian markets with a robust seafood selection have a bin of live frogs, which the fishmonger will swiftly kill and clean. Grill them, chop them, and warm them in the soup. ◊ *serves 2 to 4*

◊ ◊ ◊

4 or more wooden
toothpicks, soaked in
tepid water for 30 minutes,
if using banana leaf

A Thai granite mortar
and pestle

A grill, preferably charcoal
(highly recommended),
grate oiled

Paste

6 makhwen

3 g coriander seeds

2 g / 4 dried long peppers

2 (12 by 9-inch / 30 by
23-cm) pieces fresh or
thawed frozen banana
leaf, each halved crosswise
(optional)

33 g pickled gouramy
fish fillets

34 g Kapi Kung
(Homemade shrimp paste),
page 238

25 g stemmed dried
Mexican puya chiles

37 g peeled Asian shallots,
thinly sliced against the
grain

Make the paste

Combine the makhwen, coriander seeds, and long peppers in a small pan and set over low heat. Cook, stirring and tossing often, until the spices are very fragrant and the coriander seeds turn a shade or two darker, about 5 minutes. Transfer to a small bowl.

If using the banana leaf, stack the halves of 1 piece. Alternatively, create a double layer of aluminum foil of about the same size. Put the gouramy fillets on the center of the banana leaf or foil, fold in the sides to make a packet, and secure closed with the toothpicks if using banana leaf. Enclose the shrimp paste in a second packet the same way, using the remaining banana leaf halves or a double layer of foil. Wipe the small pan you used for the spices clean, set it over medium heat (or better yet, grill it over a low charcoal fire), add the packets, and cook, turning the packets over occasionally, until you can smell the floral funk of the gouramy and shrimp paste, about 15 minutes.

Open the gouramy packet, discard any large bones and fins (don't try to remove the small bones), and transfer the remainder to the mortar. Firmly pound until a fine paste forms and the bones have fully broken down, about 45 seconds. Scoop the paste into a bowl. Open the shrimp paste packet and add the shrimp paste to the bowl.

Add the chiles to the mortar and pound firmly, occasionally stopping to scrape the mortar and stirring the mixture once or twice, until you have a fairly fine powder, about 5 minutes. Add the spice mixture and pound to a coarse powder, about 1 minute. Add the shallots and pound until fairly smooth, about 1 minute. Add the gouramy and shrimp paste and pound just until they are fully incorporated and you have a coarse, dryish paste with visible flecks of spices, about 30 seconds.

You'll have about 130 g / ½ cup paste. You can use it right away, or you can store it in an airtight container in the fridge for up to 1 week or in the freezer for up to 6 months.

Make the soup

Prepare the grill to cook with medium heat (see page 129). Lightly season the frog legs all over with salt and grill, flipping once, until just cooked through, 5 to 7 minutes. Cut the pairs into individual legs.

Heat the oil over medium-low heat in a heavy pot until it shimmers. Add 16 g / 2 tablespoons of the paste and the garlic and cook, stirring frequently, until the garlic lightly browns, about 3 minutes.

Meanwhile, lightly smash the lemongrass with a pestle, a pan, or the flat surface of a knife blade, then cut enough crosswise on the diagonal into slices ¼ inch / 6 mm thick to yield 12 g / 2 tablespoons. Add the lemongrass, stock, fish sauce, and galangal to the pot. Tear the lime leaves and add them, too. Increase the heat to high and bring to a boil. Immediately lower the heat to maintain a gentle simmer, add the shallots and cook until they are tender, about 3 minutes. Add the frog legs and cook until warmed through. Let cool slightly, then taste and adjust the seasoning with fish sauce.

Spoon the soup into a serving bowl, then sprinkle on the green onions, sawtooth herb, cilantro, and dill. Serve right away.

Soup

6 pairs fresh or thawed frozen frog legs, patted dry

Kosher salt

2 tablespoons Naam Man Krathiam (Fried garlic oil), page 234

14 g / 2 tablespoons thinly sliced garlic

1 large stalk lemongrass, bottom 1 inch / 2.5 cm, top 9 inches / 23 cm, and outer layer removed

3 cups / 700 ml Sup Kraduuk Muu (Thai pork stock), page 241

1 tablespoon Thai fish sauce

18 g / 2 tablespoons thinly sliced (⅛ inch / 3 mm) peeled fresh or thawed frozen galangal

2 g / 3 large fresh or frozen makrut lime leaves

2 ounces / ½ cup peeled small Asian shallots or red pearl onions, halved lengthwise if large

10 g / 2 tablespoons sliced (¼ inch / 6 mm) green onions

4 g / 2 tablespoons thinly sliced sawtooth herb

4 g / 2 tablespoons coarsely chopped cilantro (thin stems and leaves)

3 g / 2 tablespoons coarsely chopped fresh dill

TOM SAEP MUU

ต้มแซ่บหมู   Isaan sour soup with pork

Just about everyone has encountered *tom yam*. It's practically illegal for Thai restaurants in America to exclude it from their menus. At its best, it's an excellent soup, sour, sweet, and spicy, typically in that order, and often bobbing with shrimp and mushrooms. At the risk of generalizing, *tom yam* is a Central Thai dish. The North has its renditions, such as Tom Som Kai Baan (Sour Northern Thai "village chicken" soup), page 57, as does the Northeast, where *tom saep* originates.

Although the concept is the same—all three are variants of sour, spicy soup—*tom saep* (in the Isaan language, *tom* means "boiled" and *saep* means "tasty") differs in several ways from the most familiar species. First, sweetness is virtually nonexistent. A touch of sugar just barely tempers the soup's bracing tartness, which can come from ingredients like lime, tamarind leaves, or sour tomatoes. Second, *tom saep* is not just spicy but incendiary, enough to bring sweat to the brow and perhaps a tear to the eye. Third, the protein of choice is often pork, beef, or water buffalo—in particular, stomach, tendon, and organs, their gamy flavor tamed by the aromatics in the broth. (The version I provide here, however, is extremely fancy in that it includes plenty of muscle.) The soup goes especially well with whiskey, whether top shelf or rotgut, because its sweetness provides a nice contrast to soup.   ◊ *serves 2 to 4*

◊ ◊ ◊

SPECIAL EQUIPMENT

A Thai granite mortar and pestle

Offal

8 ounces / 225 g pork offal (a mixture of liver, trimmed heart, and intestines), cut into about 2-inch / 5-cm pieces

Several dashes of Thai fish sauce

3 cups / 720 ml water

Soup

4 ounces / 115 g boneless pork shoulder

10 g / 10 cilantro roots

1 g / ½ teaspoon black peppercorns

Less than 1 g / ¼ teaspoon kosher salt

1 stalk lemongrass, bottom 1 inch / 2.5 cm, top 9 inches / 23 cm, and outer layer removed

18 g / 12 stemmed fresh Thai chiles

5 g / 6 large fresh or frozen makrut lime leaves

4 ounces / 115 g peeled small Asian shallots or red pearl onions, halved lengthwise (about ½ cup)

45-g / 3 by 1-inch / 7.5 by 2.5-cm piece peeled fresh or thawed frozen galangal, thinly sliced against the grain

¼ cup / 60 ml Thai fish sauce

8 g / 2 teaspoons granulated sugar

3 cups / 720 ml Sup Kraduuk Muu (Thai pork stock), page 241, or water

(continued)

Cook the offal

Combine the offal, fish sauce, and water in a small pot, set over high heat, and bring to a strong simmer. Check the liver. Once it's cooked through (firm and just barely pink in the center), transfer it to a cutting board. Decrease the heat to maintain a gentle but steady simmer and cook, skimming off any surface scum, just until the heart is fully cooked and the intestines are tender with some chew, about 20 minutes. Transfer the heart and intestines to the cutting board with the liver. Discard the cooking liquid. Thinly slice all of the offal into bite-size pieces. Set aside.

Make the soup

Using a very sharp knife, cut the pork against the grain into slices about 2 by 1 inch / 5 by 2.5 cm and ⅛ inch / 3 mm thick. Set aside.

Combine the cilantro roots, peppercorns, and salt in the mortar and pound until coarsely crushed, 15 to 30 seconds. Lightly smash the lemongrass with a pestle, a pan, or the flat surface of a knife blade, then cut crosswise on the diagonal into slices about ¼ inch / 6 mm thick. Lightly smash the chiles, then cut crosswise on the diagonal into slices about ½ inch / 12 mm thick. Twist the lime leaves to bruise and break them slightly.

Combine 2 teaspoons of the cilantro root paste (discarding the rest), lemongrass, chiles, makrut lime leaves, shallots, galangal, fish sauce, sugar, and stock in a saucepan, set over high heat, and bring to a boil. Add the pork shoulder, let the liquid return to a simmer, and cook until the pork is just cooked through, about 1 minute. Add the offal and lime juice, return to a simmer, and then turn off the heat.

Let the soup cool slightly. Taste and adjust the seasoning with lime juice and fish sauce. Transfer to a serving bowl, sprinkle on the sawtooth herb and green onions and serve right away.

¼ cup / 60 ml fresh lime juice, preferably from Key limes or from regular (Persian) limes spiked with a small squeeze of Meyer lemon juice

4 g / 2 tablespoons thinly sliced sawtooth herb

10 g / 2 tablespoons sliced (¼ inch / 6 mm) green onions

Tom: Soup

TOM SOM KAI BAAN

Sour Northern Thai "village chicken" soup ต้มส้มไก่บ้าน

Of all of the killer food at Laap Kai Santitham, a neighborhood joint in Chiang Mai, it's the least conspicuous dish that gets most of my attention. Newcomers will understandably be drawn to the restaurant's namesake, chicken minced and cooked with a bunch of dried spices and finished with fried garlic and shallots, or the pork ribs, bathed in hot oil and crowned with a thatch of fried lemongrass. I am, too. Yet *tom som kai baan,* though less visually arresting, is no less worth ordering.

It's sour soup of the kind you find in Northern Thailand, and it is as culturally and culinarily connected to this distinct region of the country as *tom yam* is to Central Thailand and *tom saep* to the Northeast. Each kind is the same in concept but exemplifies the flavor profile embedded in the palates of the people who live there. *Tom som,* for example, is invigoratingly spicy, crammed with aromatics and herbs, and made tart by the souring agents like tamarind leaves common in local kitchens. (In this recipe, you'll notice the presence of tomatillos, which join sweet Western tomatoes to replicate the tartness of the tomatoes grown in Thailand.) At Laap Kai Santitham and places like it, the soup is anchored by the flavor extracted from *kai baan* (village chicken), the sort of lean, scrawny birds that roam freely around backyards in the countryside.

◊ ◊ ◊

Broth

1 large stalk lemongrass, bottom 1 inch / 2.5 cm, top 9 inches / 23 cm, and outer layer removed

2½-ounce / 75-g piece (4½ by 1 inch / 11.5 by 2.5 cm) unpeeled fresh or thawed frozen galangal

1 (2- to 3-pound / 900 g to 1.4 kg) fresh or thawed frozen lean stewing chicken, preferably head and feet on

18 g / 2 tablespoons kosher salt

Although the soup may not look like much, it is the true star of the table, especially when your objective is drinking not dinner. Because *tom som kai baan* is all about the broth, you won't fill up on it. It provides a ton of flavor, heat, and an enthralling fragrance, entertaining the lot of you as bottles empty and the night goes by.

◊ *serves 12 to 16*

Make the broth

Cut the lemongrass crosswise into a few pieces, then lightly smash it and the galangal with a pestle, a pan, or the flat surface of a knife blade. Transfer to a narrow pot and add the chicken, salt, and enough water just to cover the chicken.

Set the pot over high heat and bring the water to a strong simmer. Partially cover the pot, decrease the heat to maintain a steady simmer, and cook until the meat twists off easily from the bone and the legs and wings start to separate from the body, about 1½ hours. Remove from the heat and transfer the chicken to a large plate or sheet pan.

When the chicken is cool enough to handle, pull the skin and meat (and if you're Thai, the cartilage) from the bones and tear them into bite-size shreds. Discard the bones. Pour or strain the cooking liquid into a second pot, leaving the solids behind, then add the chicken to the broth. Alternatively, you can store the broth and chicken together in an airtight container in the fridge for up to 3 days.

Make the soup

Lightly smash the lemongrass with a pestle, a pan, or the flat surface of a knife blade, then cut crosswise on the diagonal into slices about ¼ inch / 6 mm thick. Lightly smash the chiles (they should split open) and cilantro roots.

Transfer the lemongrass, chiles, cilantro roots, galangal, turmeric, fish sauce, and sugar to the pot with the chicken and broth. Set the pot over high heat and bring the mixture to a boil. Add the tomatoes, tomatillos, tamarind leaves, celery, and lime juice and cook for 1 minute.

Let it cool slightly, then taste and adjust the seasoning with fish sauce. Transfer the soup to a serving bowl. Sprinkle on the sawtooth herb, green onions, and cilantro and serve right away.

Soup

2 large stalks lemongrass, bottom 1 inch / 2.5 cm, top 9 inches / 23 cm, and outer layer removed

1½ ounces / 45 g / 30 stemmed fresh green Thai chiles

45 g / 45 cilantro roots

75 g / 1½ cups thinly sliced (⅛ inch / 3 mm) peeled fresh or thawed frozen galangal

25 g / 3 tablespoons thinly sliced (⅛ inch / 3 mm) peeled fresh or thawed frozen yellow turmeric root

¼ cup plus 1 tablespoon / 80 ml Thai fish sauce

40 g / 3 tablespoons plus 1 teaspoon granulated sugar

14 ounces / 400 g plum tomatoes (4 medium), cored and each cut into 6 wedges

10½ ounces / 280 g tomatillos (4 large), husked, well rinsed, and each cut into 6 wedges

6 ounces / 170 g fresh or frozen young tamarind leaves or chopped fresh sorrel

14 g / generous ½ cup, very coarsely chopped Chinese celery (thin stems and leaves)

½ cup plus 2 tablespoons / 150 ml fresh lime juice, preferably from Key limes or from regular (Persian) limes spiked with a small squeeze of Meyer lemon juice

6 g / 3 tablespoons thinly sliced sawtooth herb

15 g / 3 tablespoons sliced (¼ inch / 6 mm) green onions

6 g / 3 tablespoons coarsely chopped cilantro (thin stems and leaves)

NAAM PHRIK

CHILE DIPS

น้ำพริก

NAAM PHRIK TAA DAENG

Red-eye chile dip น้ำพริกตาแดง

For one reason or another, *naam phrik taa daeng* hasn't made much of a showing Stateside. Yet if you've done even minor exploration of the roadhouses of Northern Thailand, you've probably encountered the dense, deep-red paste of grilled dried chiles, garlic, and both dehydrated and fermented fish.

It's not exclusively a drinking food. In the village of Baan Mai, my friend Sunny's childhood home, the paste had a near-permanent place in the pantry. He'd eat some with sticky rice after school, the way an American kid might slather peanut butter on a slice of bread. But me, I eat it most often at those venues that sell little more than bottles of beer and a collection of animal parts pulled from murky bubbling oil. Served in a judicious lump on a small plate, this *naam phrik* is exhilaratingly spicy (*taa daeng* means "red eye" and refers to one supposed effect of eating the dip), umami rich, and salty with an undercurrent of funk, perfect for igniting the flavor of fried flesh as well as that of its other standard partners, like steamed cabbage, pickled mustard greens, boiled eggs, pork cracklings, and sticky rice.

◊ *Makes ¾ cup / 180 ml*

◊ ◊ ◊

SPECIAL EQUIPMENT

A grill, preferably charcoal (highly recommended), grate oiled

4 or more wooden toothpicks, soaked in tepid water for 30 minutes, if using banana leaf

3 wooden skewers, soaked in tepid water for 30 minutes

A Thai granite mortar and pestle

---

1 (12 by 9-inch / 30 by 23-cm) piece fresh or thawed frozen banana leaf, halved crosswise (optional)

1¼ ounces / 35 g pickled gouramy fish fillets

25 g stemmed dried Mexican puya chiles

3½ ounces / 100 g unpeeled Asian shallots

1 (1¾-ounce / 50-g) unpeeled garlic head

20 g dried meaty whole fish, 4 to 10 inches / 10 to 25 cm long

1 g / ½ teaspoon kosher salt

Thai fish sauce, for seasoning

To Serve Alongside

Steamed vegetables, such as white cabbage, kabocha squash, long beans, and eggplant

Khaep Muu (Pork cracklings), page 107

Khao Niaw (Sticky rice), page 248, optional

Prepare the grill to cook with medium heat (see page 129).

If you're using the banana leaf, stack the halves. Alternatively, create a double layer of aluminum foil of about the same size. Put the gouramy fillets on the center of the banana leaf or foil, fold the sides in to make a packet, and secure closed with the toothpicks if using banana leaf. Thread the chiles and the shallots through their narrow sides (so they will lay flat on the grill) onto the skewers.

Put the gouramy packet, chiles, shallots, garlic, and dried fish on the grill grate and grill, transferring them to a plate as they are ready: Cook the chiles, turning them frequently, until they turn dark brown (but not black) and have a tobaccoey smell, about 3 to 5 minutes. Cook the fish packet, turning it frequently, just until you can smell the floral funk of the gouramy, about 15 minutes. Cook the dried fish, turning occasionally, until it turns golden brown, smells toasty, and is brittle throughout, about 15 minutes. Cook the garlic and shallots, turning them frequently, until the skin is charred in spots and they are fully soft but still hold their shape, 15 to 25 minutes. Let everything cool to room temperature.

Combine the chiles and salt in the mortar and pound firmly, occasionally stopping to scrape down the sides of the mortar and stirring the mixture once or twice, until you have a coarse powder, about 3 minutes. Add the dried fish and pound, stirring once or twice, to a fairly fine powder, about 2 minutes.

Open the gouramy packet, discard any large bones and fins (don't try to remove the small bones), and transfer the remainder to the mortar. Firmly pound until the bones have fully broken down, about 45 seconds.

Peel the shallots and garlic (but don't be obsessive about it). Add the garlic to the mortar and pound to a thick, fairly fine sludge, about 30 seconds. Add the shallots and do the same, about 1 minute.

Gradually add just enough water (no more than 2 tablespoons) to loosen the paste, stirring with the pestle to incorporate. The texture should be slightly thicker than that of tomato paste. Taste, then gradually mix in just enough fish sauce to give the paste a nice umami kick.

Serve the dip right away with the suggested accompaniments, or store it in an airtight container in the fridge for up to several weeks. For future use, bring the dip to room temperature before serving.

NAAM PHRIK KHAA

Galangal chile dip   น้ำพริกข่า

Thai food has no rules, or at least none without exceptions. Curries can be as thin as broth or as thick as gravy. Noodle soups can be ordered without soup. And *naam phrik,* which is a culinary category that literally translates as "chile water," is not always wet.

Naam phrik khaa shares this latter category with many other chile-based relishes that range from soupy dips to thick pastes. *Naam phrik khaa* begins as a paste of garlic, lemongrass, dried chiles, and the slightly citrusy namesake rhizome *khaa* (galangal). The paste is cooked in a dry wok until every last bit of moisture has evaporated, and what's left is a coarse, fiber-flecked powder. A common sight on beer-cluttered tables in the North, the distinctive dip is commonly eaten with steamed oyster mushrooms, steamed beef, or *Jin Tup* (Hammered flank steak), page 135, flank steak marinated with salt and MSG, slowly grilled, and then whacked to shreds with a sledgehammer. You grab some mushroom, meat, or sticky rice, dab it in the powder, and eat.

For restaurants that traffic in the stuff, making enough to meet demand is no small task. I've seen sweat-soaked cooks pound the paste in waist-high mortars. I've watched them keep vigil beside giant woks set over glowing charcoal, wielding shovel-size spatulas to stir constantly. At home, the cook's job is much less grueling because you'll be making a small portion (a little *naam phrik khaa* goes a long way). And in yet another exception

◊ ◊ ◊

---

15 g stemmed dried
Mexican puya chiles

1 g kosher salt

14 thinly sliced lemongrass
(tender parts only), from
about 2 large stalks

2¼ ounces / 65 g peeled
fresh or thawed frozen
galangal, thinly sliced
against the grain

1¼ ounces /35 g peeled
garlic cloves, halved
lengthwise

To Serve Alongside

Steamed oyster mushrooms
and/or Jin Tup (Hammered
flank steak), page 135

Khao Niaw (Sticky rice),
page 248, optional

¾ cup / 180 ml Naam
Makham Piak (Tamarind
water), page 236

14 g / ¼ cup Naam Phrik
Khaa (Galangal chile dip),
page 67

6 g / 1½ teaspoons
granulated sugar

Less than 1 g / ⅛ teaspoon
kosher salt

to the rule, and after all that effort spent drying it out, *naam phrik khaa* is sometimes mixed with tamarind water and served right beside a separate little dish of the powder. Go figure. ◊ *makes about 35 g / ½ cup*

Combine the chiles and salt in the mortar and pound firmly, occasionally stopping to scrape down the sides of the mortar and stirring the mixture once or twice, until you have a fairly fine powder, about 5 minutes. Add the lemongrass and pound, again stopping occasionally to scrape down the sides of the mortar, until you have a fairly smooth, fibrous paste, about 2 minutes. Do the same with the galangal, about 4 minutes, and then with the garlic, about 3 minutes, fully pounding each ingredient before moving on to the next. You'll have about 135 g / ½ cup paste.

Next, you're going to cook the paste slowly in a dry wok until all of the moisture has evaporated and a completely dry, coarse powder remains. The trick is to use very low heat (if you can't get your heat low enough, try removing the wok from the burner occasionally) and, in this case, a nonstick surface. A wooden wok spatula will allow you to scrape the pan without scratching it.

Preheat the wok over very low heat. Add all of the paste and cook, stirring constantly, breaking up even small clumps where moisture might be lurking, and scraping the pan often to make sure the paste doesn't clump or burn, until the paste has transformed into a very coarse, completely dry mixture, 30 to 50 minutes.

Transfer the mixture to a shallow bowl or plate and let cool completely. Serve right away with the suggested accompaniments, or store in an airtight container at room temperature for up to 2 weeks.

DIPPING SAUCE VERSION

◊ *makes about ¾ cup / 180 ml*

Combine the tamarind water, chile dip, sugar, and salt in a small bowl and stir well.

NAAM PHRIK NUM

Green chile dip　น้ำพริกหนุ่ม

On a table crammed with sticky rice, soups, stir-fries, grilled meat, steamed vegetables, and perhaps a few beers, this Northern Thai *naam phrik* (essentially, chile-based dip) is part of a proper meal. But take away most of those other dishes, add a heap of fried meat, and triple the number of bottles, and *naam phrik* is quintessential *aahaan kap klaem*.

The dip's dual role embodies the blurry line separating drinking food from food that you happen to eat along with some drinks. Whatever the purpose, this dip is worth your attention. It's powerful stuff, a coarse, pulpy paste made from green chiles called *phrik num* that are grilled and pounded along with garlic, shallots, and fermented fish. In the boozing context, it tends to be dolloped without ceremony on plates at spots that specialize in deep-fried foods—dainty chicken drumsticks, sun-dried bits of beef, pork belly, and the like. Swiping its common partners (sticky rice, pork cracklings, steamed cabbage, pickled mustard greens, and simple boiled eggs) through the unassuming mush electrifies each bite with the grassy flavor of the headlining chile as well as its lip-tingling heat.

Although the specific chile doesn't show up Stateside, I've been successfully jury-rigging its flavor using Anaheim, Hungarian wax, or goat horn chiles, plus some serranos, if necessary, for extra heat. ◊ ***Makes about 1 cup / 240 ml***

◊ ◊ ◊

A grill, preferably charcoal (highly recommended), grate oiled

4 or 5 wooden skewers, soaked in tepid water for 30 minutes

4 or more wooden toothpicks, soaked in tepid water for 30 minutes, if using banana leaf

A Thai granite mortar and pestle

---

2 ounces / 55 g unpeeled Asian shallots

1 ounce / 30 g unpeeled garlic cloves

Several stemmed fresh green Thai or serrano chiles (if necessary)

8 ounces / 225 g small stemmed green Anaheim, Hungarian wax, or goat horn chiles

1 (12 by 9-inch / 30 by 23-cm) piece fresh or thawed frozen banana leaf, halved crosswise (optional)

1 ounce / 30 g pickled gouramy fish fillets

7 g cilantro roots

1 teaspoon Thai fish sauce

To Serve Alongside

Steamed vegetables, such as white cabbage, kabocha squash, long beans, and eggplant

Khaep Muu (Pork cracklings), page 107

Khao Niaw (Sticky rice), page 248, optional

Prepare the grill to cook with medium-high heat (see page 129).

Thread the shallots, garlic, and Thai chiles onto separate skewers. There's no need to skewer the larger chiles. If using the banana leaf, stack the halves. Alternatively, create a double layer of aluminum foil of about the same size. Put the gouramy fillets on the center of the banana leaf or foil, fold in the sides to make a packet, and secure closed with the toothpicks if using banana leaf.

Put all of the chiles on the grill grate and grill, turning them frequently and occasionally pressing them so they cook evenly, until they are completely blistered and almost completely blackened all over and the flesh is fully soft, 5 to 8 minutes for the smaller chiles and 15 to 25 minutes for the larger ones.

Raise the height of the grill grate and flatten the bed of coals, or let the coals cool slightly to cook with medium heat. Put the gouramy packet, shallots, and garlic on the grill grate and grill, transferring them to a plate as they are ready: Cook the gouramy packet, turning it occasionally, just until you can smell the floral funk of the gouramy, about 15 minutes. Cook the shallots and garlic, turning them occasionally, until they are charred in spots and fully soft but still hold their shape, 15 to 25 minutes.

While the shallots and garlic finish grilling, open the gouramy packet, discard any large bones and fins (don't try to remove the small bones), and transfer the remainder to the mortar. Firmly pound to a fine paste and the bones have fully broken down, about 45 seconds. Remove all but 1 teaspoon of the gouramy paste from the mortar, reserving it for another purpose.

Peel the grilled chiles, shallots, and garlic (but don't be too obsessive about it). Add the cilantro roots to the gouramy in the mortar and pound to a coarse paste, about 30 seconds. Add the garlic to the mortar and pound to a fairly fine paste, about 2 minutes. Do the same with the shallots, about 2 minutes.

Taste the large cooked chiles. If the heat level is too high, remove some or all of their seeds. If the heat level is too low, gradually supplement with the Thai chiles. Add the chiles to the mortar and pound until they break down into long, thin strands (don't mash them to a fine paste), 1 to 2 minutes. Add the fish sauce and pound briefly to incorporate it.

Serve right away with the suggested accompaniments, or store in an airtight container in the fridge for up to 3 days. Bring to room temperature before serving.

BIA

Beer

เบียร์

Three men, gathered around a stone table in Chiang Mai, are laughing at a scorpion. They're at a tiny open-air corner store, the Chiang Mai equivalent of a bodega, that functions as a makeshift bar at night. It is a familiar scene in Thailand, where virtually any space can become a bar as long as there's a place to loiter. This particular place has no signs or banners screaming the name of booze brands or girls in high heels and short skirts hawking 100 Pipers or Chang beer that you see at the city's more prosperous pubs with a more prosperous clientele. Instead, it has just a few mismatched chairs and a visiting golden retriever named Lion. The only indication that this is a bar is a wooden rack on a table with four bottles of the gnarly distilled rice liquor called *lao khao* and some tall bottles of beer in a small fridge. The scorpion had the misfortune to roam into this bar. One of the men, brave from liquor, corners the creature and manages to pull off its stinger to cheers from his buddies.

These men are Burmese. More specifically, they belong to the Tai Yai, or Shan, ethnicity, who make up the manual labor force of Northern Thailand these days. Notably, they're not drinking beer. They explain why they're instead passing around a bottle of *lao khao*, most of which is already gone. They're laborers who work long hours for not much pay, and they're ready for a little fun. While they vastly prefer the taste of beer, by comparison, it is wildly expensive and weak. *Lao khao* might be harsh, but a big bottle costs sixty-five baht and gets the job done.

Nearly everywhere else I've traveled in the world, beer has been the poor man's drink. Not in Thailand. To find out more about beer's place in Thai culture, I spoke to Nick Bhirombhakdi. In 1933, his grandfather, Phraya Bhirombhakdi, started Boon Rawd Brewery, which produced the first beer made in Thailand. Before that, he says, you'd occasionally see beers like the Danish Carlsberg and the Japanese Sapporo, but they were almost exclusively drunk by expats. Thais drank *lao khao*.

Phraya Bhirombhakdi was an entrepreneur. In the late 1920s, before there was a bridge over the Chao Phraya River that courses through the heart of Bangkok, he ran a lucrative ferry service that took people across the river. When plans for a bridge were announced, he understood his ferry's days were numbered. So he jumped ship, selling his ferry business and using the money to travel in Germany. There he found a culture transfixed by an elixir made from fermented barley. He had an idea. He urged his brother, who was studying in Germany at the time, to ditch architecture and learn brewing instead. A few years later, they opened their first brewery, in Bangkok.

In lieu of the focus groups that rule the beer industry nowadays, Phraya and his brother ran an experiment: they brewed several types of beer, sold them under different brand names, and decided to let the market decide which one they'd keep. Singha won. But competition from the imports remained fierce. They might have thrown in the towel had King Rama VII not visited the brewery and granted them use of the national emblem on the label. Even more significant, perhaps, the king reduced the tax on locally brewed beer, effectively increasing the price of the imports.

Still, beer was a premium product. Nick's grandfather traveled to the provinces—deep into *lao khao* territory—to proselytize his product, bringing a projector to show movies outdoors and selling beer. As other Thai companies came out with beers and sold them cheaply, the Singha company launched budget brands that have stuck around, including Leo and Thai.

Thriftier options haven't helped beer eclipse *lao khao* among the working class, however. It remains a drink for the well-to-do and the burgeoning middle class, or for celebration, to be cracked open in good times like Champagne is in the States. It's the focus at German-style beer halls, where you'll drink *Hefeweizen* and *Dunkel* from mugs and find straight-up attempts at sausage, mainstream Thai drinking food, and odd, awesome fusions, such as deep-fried pork knuckle served with chile sauce, mashed potatoes, and sauerkraut. Recently, it has become fashionable for those among the *hi-so* (the prevailing Thai slang for "high society") set to ditch whiskey for imported craft beer and other top-shelf suds from heritage breweries in Europe, where a pint fetches as much as a farmworker makes in a day. That's not to say you see it only in spiffy bars. It's on offer at city bars both modern and ramshackle, and in countryside saloons and convenience stores, too.

Unlike in the West, in Thailand beers like Singha are typically drunk over ice, a custom that Nick says dates to the days before refrigeration was widely available. (Presumably ice was a luxury then, which further underscores beer's high-class status at the time.) The appeal is immediately clear to anyone who's sweated his way through a trip to Thailand, even during the cool season. Order beer at a bar or restaurant and tall bottles almost invariably arrive with a bucket of ice and tongs. Friends fill one another's glasses with cubes, though often the task falls to beer girls, the comely young women hired by beer companies to hustle their brands and who essentially become your drink waitresses for the evening.

Nowadays, some bars—including Whiskey Soda Lounge—take the concept and run with it, offering a low-tech example of molecular gastronomy known as *bia wun*—literally "jelly beer" and essentially a beer slushie.

KHAWNG THAWT

FRIED FOODS

ของทอด

LAAP MUU THAWT

Fried minced pork patties   ลาบหมูทอด

I'm not a big believer in authenticity. I've found that what's authentic to one person is sacrilege to another just the next town over. Still, I have learned to value what's old and be skeptical of the new. That's why I had fairly low expectations for a dish called *laap thawt* that I first heard about while researching this book.

Laap, for those of you not familiar with my previous ramblings, is a dish of vividly seasoned finely chopped meat with nearly infinite variations that essentially cleave between the Northern versions and the Northeastern versions. All you need to know for our purposes here is that of the thousands of renditions of *laap* I'd eaten, exactly zero had been served *thawt* (deep-fried). I smelled a novelty dish, the Thai equivalent of the Cronut.

Sure, new doesn't always mean bad. Yet so many of my favorite foods in Thailand are made by people taught to cook by their mothers and grandmothers, each dish the product of several generations' worth of knowledge. When people deem something "authentic," I think what they mean is that it is rooted to a place with its own history and hard-won culinary logic. Without that foundation, you can end up with mystifyingly trendy items such as the *som tam* platter, a tray of papaya salad surrounded by herbs, hot dogs, pork balls, and pork rinds, among other things, that are good separately but (to me, at least) are bizarre together.

◊ ◊ ◊

Paste

30 g unpeeled garlic cloves

30 g unpeeled Asian shallots

14 g piece peeled fresh or thawed frozen galangal, cut against the grain into slices ¼ inch (6 mm) thick

Patties

1 pound / 455 g ground pork

3 tablespoons plus 1 teaspoon / 50 ml fresh lime juice, preferably from Key limes or from regular (Persian) limes spiked with a small squeeze of Meyer lemon juice

3 tablespoons plus 1 teaspoon / 50 ml Thai fish sauce

19 g / 2 tablespoons plus 1 teaspoon Khao Khua (Toasted–sticky rice powder), page 232

12 g / 2½ teaspoons granulated sugar

10 g / 1 heaping tablespoon thinly sliced lemongrass (tender parts only), from about 2 large stalks

10 g / 2 tablespoons sliced (¼ inch / 6 mm) green onions

8 g / ¼ cup coarsely chopped cilantro (thin stems and leaves)

(continued)

My skepticism of *laap thawt* only deepened when a friend convinced me that my first taste of it should be at a Bangkok bar called Tuba, a multiroom establishment adorned with colorful retro furniture, wacky chandeliers, and objets d'art like giant Hulk and Yoda statues. Frankly, the place *looks* awesome. But when my friends and I were handed menus wrapped in what looked like Hugh Hefner's old velvet smoking jackets, I gave up full stop on having anything good to eat.

Well, we ate a bunch of dishes that night, most of them killer. The standout, of course, was a plate of minced pork seasoned like Northeastern-style *laap* (with lime juice, fish sauce, chile powder, and toasted-rice powder), then formed into patties and browned in hot oil. ◊ *serves 4 to 6*

Make the paste

Prepare the grill to cook with medium heat (see page 129), or preheat a stove-top grill pan over medium heat. If you're using a grill, thread the garlic and shallots onto separate skewers. Put the garlic, shallots, and galangal on the grill grate or the grill pan and cook, transferring them to a plate as they are ready: Cook the galangal slices, turning them once or twice, until they are cooked through and the slices look dry on both sides (don't let them char or brown), about 5 minutes. Cook the garlic and shallots, turning them once or twice, until the skin is charred in spots and they are fully soft but still hold their shape, 15 to 25 minutes. Let them cool to room temperature.

Pound the galangal in the mortar to a fairly smooth, fibrous paste, about 1 minute. Peel the garlic, add to the mortar, and pound until fully incorporated, 1 to 2 minutes. Do the same with the shallots and pound to a fairly smooth, slightly fibrous paste, 2 to 3 minutes.

You will have about 32 g / ¼ cup paste. You can use it right away, or it will keep in an airtight container in the fridge for up to 1 week or in the freezer for up to 6 months. Measure out 16 g / 2 tablespoons of the paste for the patties and put it in a large bowl; reserve the remainder for another use.

Make the patties

Add all of the ingredients for the patties to the paste in the bowl and use your hand to mix and squish the ingredients until they are evenly combined. Then continue mixing and squishing until the mixture is slightly sticky, about 2 minutes. Cover and refrigerate until chilled, about 15 minutes.

To shape each patty, grab 1½ ounces / 45 g of the mixture, roll it between your palms into a rough sphere (about the size of a golf ball), and then flatten the ball to form a ½-inch- / 12-mm-thick patty.

Fry and serve the patties

Select a heavy pot at least 12 inches / 30 cm wide and pour in the oil to a depth of 2 to 3 inches / 5 to 7.5 cm. Set the pot over high heat and heat the oil to 350°F / 180°C. Use the thermometer to test the temperature, measuring the oil at the center of the vessel and carefully stirring the oil occasionally to ensure a consistent temperature. Line a large sheet pan with paper towels or newspaper and set it near the stove.

While the oil is heating, stir together the rice flour and tempura batter mix in a large, shallow bowl.

Fry the patties in several batches to avoid crowding the oil: One by one, add a patty to the flour mixture, turn to coat it with a thin layer, tap off the excess, and then carefully add it to the hot oil. Cook the patties, turning them if necessary to cook evenly, until golden brown and crispy, about 3 minutes. Using the spider or a slotted spoon, transfer the patties to the prepared pan to drain. Repeat until all of the patties are fried.

Serve the patties on a plate with the cabbage and chiles alongside (to eat between bites of the patties). Sprinkle on the cilantro and serve right away.

4 g / 2 tablespoons thinly sliced sawtooth herb

4 g / 6 large very thinly sliced fresh or frozen makrut lime leaves (stems removed if thick)

3 g / 1 generous tablespoon thinly sliced mint leaves

4 g / 1 tablespoon plus 1 teaspoon Phrik Pon Khua (Toasted-chile powder), page 233

To Finish

Neutral oil (such as soybean or palm), for deep-frying (about 12 cups / 2.8 L)

50 g / ¼ cup plus 3 tablespoons Asian white rice flour (not glutinous rice flour)

15 g / 2 tablespoons tempura batter mix, preferably Gogi brand

Several white cabbage wedges

About 12 fresh Thai chiles, red or green

About 8 g / ¼ cup very coarsely chopped cilantro (thin stems and leaves)

Pig's ears and intestines, stewed with five spice and aromatics then fried crisp. Black vinegar makes for good dipping, and optional sliced Thai chiles don't hurt.

SAI MUU / HUU MUU THAWT

ไส้หมู / หูหมูทอด   Fried chitterlings / pig's ears

Offal is common drinking fare, but not because Thais require any alcohol-induced encouragement. In Thailand, eating entrails and other odd bits of the animal isn't the trend or novelty it is in many parts of the States. And while its prevalence probably arose in times of scarcity, when wasting beef tendon and pork snout would've been borderline reckless behavior, nowadays these motley parts are relished, not just tolerated. In fact, tripe, liver, and the like make especially good partners for booze because they tend to feature the chewy, cartilaginous, and other textures that entertain the merry snacker.

Here, two of my pet parts, interchangeable in this recipe, are simmered in a salty-sweet, aromatic liquid that melds Chinese flavors like five spice, rock sugar, and soy sauce and Thai ones like galangal, lemongrass, cilantro roots, and pandan leaves, which are typically found in the Asian-supermarket freezer in the States and provide a jasmine ricelike flavor. Once they are tender, infused with flavor, and an enticing deep brown, they take a cold nap in the fridge, followed by a minute or two in hot oil until they're good and crunchy. They're great dipped in sharp, malty black vinegar, easy to find in any market with a robust Chinese sauce selection. Those new to chitterlings (small intestines of a hog) cookery be warned: they stink. What else do you expect from this stretch of the road to you know where? ◊ *serves 4 to 6*

Stew the pork

If using ears, use a razor blade to remove any lingering hairs. Lightly smash the lemongrass with a pestle, a pan, or the flat surface of a knife blade, then cut on the diagonal into slices about ¼ inch / 6 mm thick. Lightly smash the cilantro roots and the galangal.

Combine all of the stew ingredients in a large pot and bring to a boil over high heat. Turn down the heat to maintain a steady simmer and cook, stirring occasionally, until tender. Chitterlings will take about 45 minutes. Ears will take about 1½ hours (they are ready when you can easily push a finger through the skin and touch the cartilage).

Drain well, reserving the cooking liquid if you have cooked ears and discarding it if you have cooked chitterlings. Pat dry. Strain the reserved liquid and freeze for the next time you cook pig's ears.

Set a cooling rack over a large sheet pan. Arrange the chitterlings or ears in a single layer and refrigerate, uncovered, to dry, at least 8 hours or up to overnight.

If using chitterlings, cut into 1-inch / 2.5-cm lengths. If using ears, cut into slices 2 to 3 inches / 5 to 7.5 cm long and ⅛ inch / 3 mm wide.

Fry and serve the dish

Select a heavy pot at least 12 inches / 30 cm wide and pour in the oil to a depth of 2 to 3 inches / 5 to 7.5 cm. Set the pot over high heat and heat the oil to 325°F / 165°C. Use the thermometer to test the temperature, measuring the oil at the center of the vessel and carefully stirring the oil occasionally to ensure a consistent temperature. Line a large sheet pan with paper towels or newspaper and set it near the stove.

Working in batches to avoid crowding the oil, add the chitterlings or ears to the hot oil, cover with the splatter screen, and fry, stirring occasionally, until crunchy, 1 to 2 minutes. Using the spider or a slotted spoon, transfer them to the prepared pan to drain and then season lightly with salt. Repeat with the remaining chitterlings or ears.

Transfer to a plate and serve right away with a bowl of the vinegar for dipping.

SPECIAL EQUIPMENT

A deep-fry thermometer

A splatter screen

A large spider skimmer (recommended)

Stew

2½ pounds / 1.2 kg fresh or thawed frozen chitterlings or pig's ears (without the thick base), rinsed

2 large stalks lemongrass, bottom 1 inch / 2.5 cm, top 9 inches / 23 cm, and outer layer removed

30 g / 30 cilantro roots

70 g / ½ cup thinly sliced (⅛ inch / 3 mm) peeled fresh or thawed frozen galangal

60 g / 1 cup very coarsely chopped Chinese celery stems

12 cups / 2.8 L water

1½ cups / 360 ml Thai thin soy sauce

½ cup / 120 ml Thai black soy sauce

110 g / ½ cup rock sugar

14 g / 2 tablespoons ground black pepper

2 (6-g) pieces Ceylon or Mexican cinnamon (about 3 inches / 7.5 cm long)

1 g / 5 dried bay leaves, preferably from an Asian market

1 g / 3 star anise pods

55 g / 2 fresh or thawed frozen pandan leaves, tied into a knot

To Finish

Neutral oil (such as soybean or palm), for deep-frying (about 12 cups / 2.8 L)

Kosher salt

Chinese black vinegar, for dipping

Deep-fried chicken kneecaps, for the win.

EN KAI THAWT

เอ็นไก่ทอด   Fried chicken tendons

It's funny how something so common in one place can be almost unheard of in another. In Thailand, for instance, nearly anywhere that does drinking food serves *en kai thawt*, or deep-fried chicken tendons. Made up of cartilage, flesh, and I'm not sure what else, the part (technically the kneecap, as far as I can tell) is marinated, battered, twice fried, and served with sweet chile sauce, typically straight out of the bottle. This is popcorn chicken for people who like gristle and crunch.

Here in the States, the dish is a rarity at restaurants. At most butcher shops that cater to Western tastes, the chicken part in question ends up in the trash because no one asks for it. So if you're eager to make the dish, that's my suggestion: find a kindhearted butcher and ask well in advance. If the knees are a no-go, see if he or she would be willing to part with the same amount of the cartilage at the bottom of the breastbone, which you will need to chop into pieces. ◊ *serves 2 to 4*

◊ ◊ ◊

A Thai granite mortar
and pestle

A deep-fry thermometer

A large spider skimmer
(recommended)

Tendons and Marinade

8 ounces / 225 g chicken
tendons or chicken breast
cartilage

3 g / 1 peeled garlic clove,
halved lengthwise

1 teaspoon Thai fish sauce

1 teaspoon Thai seasoning
sauce (look for the
green cap)

Less than 1 g / ¼ teaspoon
chicken bouillon powder

To Finish

50 g / ¼ cup plus
3 tablespoons Asian
white rice flour (not
glutinous rice flour)

15 g / 2 tablespoons Asian
tapioca starch

15 g / 2 tablespoons
tempura batter mix,
preferably Gogi brand

½ cup plus 1 tablespoon /
135 ml Naam Boon Sai
(Limestone water),
page 240

6 g / 2 teaspoons toasted
sesame seeds

Neutral oil (such as
soybean or palm), for
deep-frying (about
12 cups / 2.8 L)

Naam Jim Kai (Sweet chile
dipping sauce), page 244,
for serving

Marinate the tendons

Rinse the tendons or cartilage and drain well. If you're using cartilage,
chop into ½-inch / 12-mm pieces.

Pound the garlic in the mortar to a fine paste, about 1 minute. Transfer
to a bowl. Add the fish sauce, seasoning sauce, and bouillon and stir well.
Add the tendons and mix well with your hands. Cover and marinate in
the fridge for at least 30 minutes or up to 1 hour.

Fry and serve the dish

Combine the rice flour, tapioca starch, tempura batter mix, limestone
water, and sesame seeds in a bowl and stir until smooth.

Select a heavy pot at least 12 inches / 30 cm wide and pour in the oil to
a depth of 2 to 3 inches / 5 to 7.5 cm. Set the pot over high heat and heat
the oil to 275°F / 135°C. Use the thermometer to test the temperature,
measuring the oil at the center of the vessel and carefully stirring the oil
occasionally to ensure a consistent temperature. Line a large sheet pan
with paper towels or newspaper and set it near the stove.

While the oil is heating, squeeze the tendons to remove excess marinade,
transfer to the batter, and toss well with your hands. When the oil is
ready, add half of the tendons, carefully introducing them to the oil in
rapid succession at the edge of the pot and adjusting the heat to maintain
a temperature of 250°F / 120°C. Wait a minute or so, then stir with the
spider or with tongs to make sure the tendons don't stick together. Continue frying, stirring and turning the tendons occasionally, until they are
light golden brown, about 5 minutes. Using the spider or a slotted spoon,
transfer the tendons to the prepared pan to drain. Cook the remaining
tendons the same way.

Increase the heat to bring the oil to 325°F / 165°C. Transfer all of the tendons to the spider or spoon and stand back as you carefully lower them
into the oil. Let them pop and crackle until they are golden brown and
very crispy, 20 to 30 seconds. Again, use the spider or spoon to transfer
the tendons to the prepared pan to drain. They will stay crunchy for up
to 45 minutes.

Transfer to a plate and serve with the dipping sauce.

NEUA / MUU DAET DIAW

Fried semidried beef / pork

เนื้อ / หมูแดดเดียว

In the food of Thailand, especially in the realm of drinking fare, chewiness is a feature, not a flaw. Yet if some well-meaning restaurateur decided to serve *neua daet diaw* at his bar in Brooklyn, he'd probably face daily customer complaints about how it's overcooked, undercooked, or other variations on "not tender enough." After a while, he might be tempted to lock himself in a closet and pull out what's left of his hair.

That's too bad because *neua daet diaw* is seriously good stuff. *Daet* means "sun" and *diaw* means "a little bit." In other words, this is meat—either *neua* (beef), *muu* (pork), or *khwai* (water buffalo)—that's been left in the sun long enough to dehydrate but not so much that it becomes like jerky. By the time *neua daet diaw* reaches your plate, it has probably been deep-fried and does indeed require the exertion of your jaw muscles. And it's better for it.

If letting meat sit out in the hot sun for several hours strikes you as unwise, let me assure you that I've eaten the result many times and I'm still here. The last-minute trip in the deep fryer should buck you up, too. That said, you could accomplish the drying step in a food dehydrator set to 145°F / 63°C. It'll take about 3½ hours for beef and 4½ hours for pork. Rotate the shelves of the dehydrator every 20 minutes or so. ◊ *serves 8 to 10*

◊ ◊ ◊

A Thai granite mortar
and pestle

2 cooling racks
and 2 sheet pans

Cheesecloth

A deep-fry thermometer

A fine-mesh skimmer
(recommended)

Meat and Marinade

2¼ pounds / 1 kg beef
chuck flap, flank steak,
or pork shoulder

20 g / 7 peeled garlic
cloves, halved lengthwise

15 g / 15 cilantro roots

4 g / 1½ teaspoons black
peppercorns

2 g / ¾ teaspoon
kosher salt

36 g / 3 tablespoons
granulated sugar

1 tablespoon plus
2 teaspoons Thai fish sauce

1 tablespoon plus
2 teaspoons Shaoxing wine

1 tablespoon plus
2 teaspoons Thai
oyster sauce

2 teaspoons Thai thin
soy sauce

2 g / 1½ teaspoons mild
Indian curry powder

5 g / 1 tablespoon
coriander seeds, preferably
from an Asian market,
cracked in a mortar

To Finish

Neutral oil (such as
soybean or palm), for
deep-frying (about
12 cups / 2.8 L)

38 g / 3 cups fresh or
thawed frozen makrut
lime leaves, patted dry

¾ cup / 180 ml Jaew
(Isaan dipping sauce),
page 245

Marinate and dry the meat

If using beef, cut it with the grain into strips about 4 inches / 10 cm long, 1 inch / 2.5 cm wide, and ⅛ to ¼ inch / 3 to 6 mm thick. If using pork, cut it with the grain into strips about 4 inches / 10 cm long, 1 inch / 2.5 cm wide, and ¼ inch / 6 mm thick. Put the meat in a bowl and set aside.

Combine the garlic, cilantro roots, peppercorns, and salt in the mortar and pound to a fairly fine paste, 1 to 2 minutes. Transfer to the bowl with the meat and rub with your hands to coat the meat evenly with the paste.

Combine the sugar, fish sauce, wine, oyster sauce, soy sauce, and curry powder in a separate small bowl. Stir to dissolve the sugar and transfer to a large resealable bag. Add the meat to the bag and seal the bag closed, forcing out as much of the air as possible. Massage the outside to make sure the meat is well coated. Marinate in the fridge for at least 1 hour or up to 2 hours.

Set each cooling rack on a sheet pan. Remove the meat from the bag and arrange it in a single layer on the racks. Sprinkle the coriander seeds evenly over the top of the meat, covering it liberally. Put the pans outside in an area of full, direct sunlight and cover completely with the cheese-cloth, tucking the cloth under the pan on all sides. Let the meat sit in the full sun, flipping the pieces once about halfway through the drying time, until dry to the touch but still pliable, 3 to 5 hours.

At this point, you can store the meat in resealable plastic bags in the fridge for up to 5 days.

Fry and serve the dish

Select a heavy pot at least 12 inches / 30 cm wide and pour in the oil to a depth of 2 to 3 inches / 5 to 7.5 cm. Set the pot over high heat and heat the oil to 325°F / 165°C. Use the thermometer to test the temperature, measuring the oil at the center of the vessel and carefully stirring the oil occasionally to ensure a consistent temperature. Line a large sheet pan with paper towels or newspaper and set it near the stove.

Fry the meat in four equal batches to avoid crowding the oil. Carefully add the first batch to the hot oil and fry until crisp and a shade or two darker, 30 seconds to 1 minute. Using the spider or a slotted spoon, transfer the meat to the prepared pan to drain. Fry the remaining meat the same way, using a fine-mesh skimmer to scoop out stray coriander seeds after each batch.

When the final batch has been removed from the oil, carefully add the lime leaves to the oil and fry, stirring occasionally, until crisp but still bright green, about 10 seconds. Transfer them to the prepared pan.

Transfer the meat and leaves to a plate and serve right away with bowls of the sauce for dipping.

KAI THAWT

Thai-style fried chicken　ไก่ทอด

I've spent years sourcing Thai herbs, jury-rigging rotisseries, and finding domestic doppelgangers for chiles that seem to exist only in Southeast Asia. In the process, I've solved many mysteries. But after managing to engineer reasonable approximations of dishes like Northern Thai frog soup and Isaan fermented sausage, I was surprised to find that one of my most enduring struggles turned out to be making fried chicken.

And not even the more complex Southern Thai–style version—rubbed with turmeric, fried, then heaped with fried garlic and shallots—which I've yet to attempt, but the straightforward, deep golden brown drums, thighs, and wings you can find at almost any place in Thailand with a vat of hot oil out front. Like the Popeye's-style breaded sort common in the West, the battered kind ubiquitous in Thailand is almost always tasty, even when it relies on a shitload of MSG and is fried to death in blackish oil. A few too many drinks in, you might hear yourself proclaiming this stuff the best you've ever tasted.

Yet what I wanted to re-create were those rare fried chicken experiences that stayed with you—the difference between the fleeting pleasure of fast food and the lasting gratification of one of those skillet joints in the American South. For a while, I couldn't accomplish either. Whenever I fried up a batch of Thai-style chicken back in the States, I ended up with a wimpy, wet crust. Problem is, unlike breading, batter creates a seal that locks in the meat's moisture. As it tries to escape, it hits crust and makes it soggy.

◊ ◊ ◊

Chicken and Marinade

4 bone-in, skin-on
chicken thighs (about
1¼ pounds / 570 g)

4 bone-in, skin-on
chicken drumsticks
(about 1 pound / 455 g)

18 g / about 6 peeled garlic
cloves, halved lengthwise

3 g / 1 teaspoon white
peppercorns (from an
Asian market)

5 g / 5 cilantro roots

1 tablespoon Thai
fish sauce

1 tablespoon Thai
seasoning sauce (look
for the green cap)

1 teaspoon kosher salt

15 g / 1 tablespoon plus
¾ teaspoon MSG (optional
but highly recommended)

So the next time I was in Thailand, I decided to return to a faithful old strategy: pay attention. Specifically, I haunted a Chiang Mai institution called Kai Thawt Thian Kheun, or "Midnight Fried Chicken." The popular late-night spot launched a second location not long ago, which, despite its name, opens at 5:30 p.m., a convenient time for certain old farts who can no longer manage to stay up late.

Just an hour or so of observation and some mild interrogation solved my chicken conundrum. For one, the cooks had scored any especially thick chicken parts with just a slit on either side of the bone. This both helps the marinade penetrate the flesh and increases the surface area, so the meat cooks more evenly and moisture evaporates more quickly. Second, they fried the chicken longer and at a lower temperature than I'm used to. All of this adds up to chicken that's a bit drier than we Westerners are typically used to, but that's super-crispy and a bit chewy—perfect for eating while drinking. And finally, seated at a table crowded with the restaurant's typical spread—*Naam Phrik Num* (Green chile dip), page 71; *Naam Phrik Taa Daeng* (Red-eye chile dip), page 63; steamed cabbage, and boiled eggs—and holding a drumstick practically the size of my thumb, I remembered how different the chicken is in Thailand. Smaller and slightly scrawnier, the birds there are also brought straight to market after they're slaughtered. Most American chickens, on the other hand, are six-pound / 3-kg monsters that are cooled in water baths, leaving customers with bloated fowl. That's where I was really going wrong.

The scoring and the lower frying temperature are easily accomplished at home in the States. The only tricky part is getting the proper bird, though it's more readily available than ever. Nowadays, you can find an alternative to the typical water-logged poultry billed as "air-chilled chicken" at most fancy-pants supermarkets, like Whole Foods. Do this and avoid behemoths, and you're golden. ◊ *serves 4 to 6*

Marinate the chicken

Turn the thighs skin side down. Using a sharp knife, cut about halfway through the flesh of each thigh on either side of and parallel to the bone. Make a lengthwise cut down to the bone on two sides of the meaty part of the drumsticks. Put the chicken in a large mixing bowl.

Combine the garlic, peppercorns, and cilantro roots in the mortar and pound to a fine paste, 1 to 2 minutes. Add the fish sauce, seasoning sauce, salt, and MSG to the mortar and stir until well combined. Transfer the mixture to the bowl with the chicken and use your hands to mix and massage the chicken to coat it evenly with the marinade. Set a cooling rack on a sheet pan. Transfer the chicken to the rack skin side down in a single layer with some space between each piece. Refrigerate, uncovered, for 2 hours.

Fry and serve the chicken

Combine the limestone water, rice flour, tapioca starch, tempura batter mix, paprika, and chicken bouillon powder in a bowl and stir until smooth. Remove the chicken from the refrigerator and pat the pieces dry. Add them to the batter, toss to coat well, and then let them sit in the batter at room temperature for at least 20 minutes or up to 1 hour.

Select a heavy pot at least 12 inches / 30 cm wide and pour in the oil to a depth of 3 inches / 7.5 cm. Set the pot over high heat and heat the oil to 300°F / 150°C. Use the thermometer to test the temperature, measuring the oil at the center of the vessel and carefully stirring the oil occasionally to ensure a consistent temperature. Line a large sheet pan with paper towels or newspaper and set it near the stove.

Fry the chicken in two batches: One piece at a time, remove 4 pieces of chicken from the batter, shaking each piece gently to let the excess batter drip off, and carefully add them to the oil. Lower the heat to bring the oil temperature down to 250°F to 275°F / 120°C to 135°C. Cook for a minute or two, then use tongs to make sure the pieces aren't sticking together. Continue to fry, turning the pieces and stirring the oil occasionally, until the outsides are golden brown and very crispy and the chicken is cooked through, about 15 minutes. Using the tongs, transfer the pieces to the prepared pan to drain. Repeat with the remaining chicken.

Serve the chicken on a plate and serve right away with the chile dip.

To Finish

1 cup / 235 ml Naam Boon Sai (Limestone water), page 240

100 g / ¾ cup plus 2 tablespoons Asian white rice flour (not glutinous rice flour)

35 g / ¼ cup plus 2 teaspoons Asian tapioca starch

30 g / ¼ cup tempura batter mix, preferably Gogi brand

1 g / ½ teaspoon mild paprika

1 g / ½ teaspoon chicken bouillon powder, such as Knorr brand (optional but highly recommended)

Neutral oil (such as soybean or palm), for deep-frying (about 12 cups / 2.8 L)

Naam Phrik Num (Green chile dip), page 71, or Naam Phrik Taa Daeng (Red-eye chile dip), page 63), for serving

Perhaps the most popular modern drinking food in Thailand is . . . French fries!

SOM TAM THAWT

Fried papaya salad   ส้มตำทอด

All of the elements of the beloved "salad" are here: the unripe papaya, the long beans, the sweet-tart-spicy dressing. But ingenious Thai cooks have riffed on the classic, whether the originator was inspired by the fritters known as *krabong*, which are sometimes made with green papaya, or simply by the fondness for deep-frying common among the Thais. The vegetation is battered and immersed in hot fat, and the dressing becomes the dipping sauce. It's modern. It's kitschy. And it's damn good. ◊ *serves 4 to 6*

◊ ◊ ◊

A Thai granite mortar

A wooden pestle

A mandoline or Kiwi brand papaya shredder (recommended)

A deep-fry thermometer

A large spider skimmer (recommended)

Dressing

36 g / ¼ cup unsalted roasted peanuts

4 g / 3 stemmed fresh Thai chiles, preferably red

2 lime wedges, each 1 inch / 2.5 cm long and wide

14 g / 2 tablespoons Kung Haeng Khua (Dry-fried dried shrimp), page 239

4 ounces / 115 g cherry tomatoes (about 8), halved, or quartered if very large

¼ cup / 60 ml Naam Jim Kai (Sweet chile dipping sauce), page 244

2 tablespoons fresh lime juice, preferably from Key limes or from regular (Persian) limes spiked with a small squeeze of Meyer lemon juice

2 tablespoons Thai fish sauce

2 tablespoons Naam Cheuam Naam Taan Piip (Palm sugar simple syrup), page 237

Make the dressing

Crush the peanuts in the mortar to Grape Nuts–size pieces. Transfer them to a bowl.

Add the chiles to the mortar and pound until they're in several pieces. Add the lime wedges and pound very lightly and briefly, just to release the juice. Add the shrimp and pound lightly, just to release their flavor. Add the tomatoes and pound lightly, just to release some juice. Add the mixture to the peanuts along with the sweet chile sauce, lime juice, fish sauce, and simple syrup. Stir well and set aside.

Make the fritters

Peel the papaya, then use the mandoline or papaya shredder or a knife to shred the fruit into irregular strips 3 to 5 inches / 7.5 to 12 cm long and ¹⁄₁₆ to ⅛ inch / 2 to 3 mm thick. Keep at it until you have 600 g / 8 cups of strips.

Select a heavy pot at least 12 inches / 30 cm wide and pour in the oil to a depth of 2 to 3 inches / 5 to 7.5 cm. Set the pot over high heat and heat the oil to 325°F / 165°C. Use the thermometer to test the temperature, measuring the oil at the center of the vessel and carefully stirring the oil occasionally to ensure a consistent temperature. Line a large sheet pan with paper towels or newspaper and set it near the stove.

While the oil is heating, in a large bowl, toss together the papaya, carrot, and long beans. In a medium bowl, combine the rice flour, tapioca starch, and tempura batter mix and stir well. Add the limestone water and stir until smooth.

Cook the fritters in batches to avoid crowding the oil: For each fritter, scoop 70 g / 1 cup of the papaya mixture into a separate small bowl, add about ¼ cup / 60 ml of the batter and a generous pinch of salt, and toss to coat. Holding the bowl close to the surface of the hot oil and using a large spoon, ease the mixture carefully into the oil. Repeat to add more fritters to the oil. Fry each batch, turning the fritters once, until light golden brown and crispy, 8 to 10 minutes. Using the spider or a slotted spoon, transfer each cluster to the prepared pan to drain. Repeat with the remaining papaya mixture and batter.

Serve the fritters on a plate, spoon on the dressing, and serve right away.

Note on Green Papaya: Called malakaw in Thai, green papaya is a variety of the fruit used when its pale green flesh is still crisp. Look for the firm, green-skinned fruit in Asian, particularly Thai and Vietnamese, markets in the produce section. To shred it for this recipe, peel the fruit, then use a mandoline, a Kiwi brand fruit and vegetable shredder, or a sharp knife to cut the flesh as directed.

Fritters

1 large green papaya (see Note)

Neutral oil (such as soybean or palm), for deep-frying (about 12 cups / 2.8 L)

3¾ ounces / 110 g peeled carrot, cut into matchsticks about 3 inches / 7.5 cm long and ⅛ inch / 3 mm thick (about 2 cups)

5½ ounces / 155 g long beans, ends trimmed and cut into 4-inch / 10-cm lengths (about 2 cups)

100 g / ¾ cups plus 2 tablespoons Asian white rice flour (not glutinous rice flour)

30 g / ¼ cup Asian tapioca starch

30 g / ¼ cup tempura batter mix, preferably Gogi brand

1 cup / 240 ml Naam Boon Sai (Limestone water), page 240

Kosher salt

Khaep muu vendor at Talaat Thanin, in Chiang Mai, frying pork skin for fun and profit.

KHAEP MUU

Pork cracklings   แคบหมูทอด

For many Americans, fried pork skins bring to mind Mississippi or Mexico, but Thais love them, too, especially the people of Northern Thailand, who call themselves *khon meuang*. They crumble pork cracklings over noodle dishes, swipe the crunchy curls through the chile-based dips called *naam phrik*, and snack on them, much as Westerners do on Doritos. The cooking process is straightforward: fry pork skin slowly until all of the fat renders and all of the water evaporates, then briefly submerge the remaining strips of pure protein in high-temperature oil so they puff. ◊ *serves 10 to 12*

◊ ◊ ◊

A meat tenderizer

Several cooling racks and sheet pans

A deep-fry thermometer

A large spider skimmer (recommended)

———

3 pounds / 1.4 kg pork skin

1 unpeeled garlic head, halved crosswise

3 tablespoons distilled white vinegar, preferably a Thai brand

27 g / 3 tablespoons kosher salt

2 g / 1 teaspoon ground white pepper (from an Asian market)

Neutral oil (such as soybean or palm), for deep-frying (about 12 cups / 2.8 L)

Naam Phrik Num (Green chile dip), page 71, for serving

The day before you cook the cracklings: Use the meat tenderizer to prick the exterior side of the pork skin in rows ¼ to ½ inch / 6 to 12 mm apart. Using half of the garlic head, rub the cut side on both sides of the skin. Sprinkle the vinegar on the same side of the skin and rub with your hands to distribute well. Sprinkle the salt and pepper on both sides of the skin.

Set the cooling racks on the sheet pans. Lay the skin on the racks and leave uncovered in the fridge to dry for at least 8 hours or up to 12 hours.

The next day: Select a heavy pot at least 12 inches / 30 cm wide and pour in the oil to a depth of 3 inches / 7.5 cm. Set the pot over high heat and heat the oil to 275°F / 135°C. Use the thermometer to test the temperature, measuring the oil at the center of the vessel and carefully stirring the oil occasionally to ensure a consistent temperature. Set a large plate near the stove.

While the oil is heating, use a sharp, sturdy knife to cut the skin into strips about 2 inches / 5 cm long and ½ inch / 12 mm wide.

Add the pork skin to the hot oil and cook, stirring almost constantly for the first 5 minutes to prevent the pieces from sticking to one another and adjusting the heat as needed to maintain an oil temperature of 250°F to 260°F / 120°C to 125°C. Continue cooking, stirring occasionally, until the bubbling has mostly subsided and most of the pieces of skin are floating, 25 to 40 minutes. Using the spider or a slotted spoon, transfer the skins to the large plate.

Increase the heat and bring the oil to 400°F / 204°C. Line a large sheet pan with paper towels or newspaper. Working in small batches to avoid crowding the oil, add the skins to the hot oil and fry until they puff and float to the surface, 10 to 15 seconds. Using the spider or a slotted spoon, transfer them to the prepared pan to drain.

Let the pork cracklings cool. Serve right away with the chile dip, or store in an airtight container in a cool, dark place (not the fridge) for up to 2 weeks.

NAEM SII KHRONG MUU

Fried sour pork ribs   แหนมซี่โครงหมู

In the early 1990s, I was living in Chiang Mai in a sort of dormitory for university students, factory workers, and low-budget travelers like myself. Sure, my room had only a fan, desk, bed, and shower with no hot water, but it cost significantly less than the backpacker hostels geared solely toward folks spending dollars, pounds, and Deutsche marks. At the time, that was what mattered. Today, the area is crushed with boutique hotels, but back then, it had a more homegrown flavor. Kafe was my local bar.

Even then, the bar was a place where customers included nearly equal parts foreign travelers, expats, and Thais—integration of this sort is rare in Chiang Mai. Like me, the *farang* came for the location, right on the moat and in the heart of the tourist ghetto, and the cold beer. But Thais, it seemed, also came for the snacks that crowded their tables as they drank. I began ordering more or less randomly from the part of the menu that didn't include spaghetti and meatballs. The most memorable item that came was *naem sii khrong muu*, billed in English as something like "fried pork ribs." As promising as that sounds, somehow the title managed to understate the appeal. The juicy, chewy meat that I gnawed from bone nubs was salty, garlicky, and amped up by the kind of sour tang you get from salami. They were holy-shit good, especially with some peanuts, raw ginger, crunchy cabbage, and whole fresh chiles on the side. I've eaten countless renditions since, but the one at Kafe remains my standard for how the dish should taste.

◊ ◊ ◊

Brief fermentation is the key to the dish, which I'd venture comes from Isaan, the Northeastern region of Thailand, though lord knows Northern folks love fermented meat, too. I'd also venture that the fermentation was an accident before it was a technique. Someone probably forgot pork and rice in the heat for a while and came back to find the flesh had soured, in a tasty way. When the fermentation is controlled by intent and salt (today it's typically the curing variety, for safety's sake), the meat is preserved. Like many culinary miracles, the result is both functional and delicious.

The pork ribs you want for this recipe are typically sold precut in Asian markets. If you buy them elsewhere, ask your butcher to cut them down to a shorter length, about 2 inches / 5 cm. ◊ *serves 10 to 12*

Note on Fermenting Meat: Several recipes in this book employ a technique that requires letting meat ferment at a relatively hot temperature. It both acts as a means of preservation and has the ancillary effect of intensifying the meat's flavor so that a small amount of it can satisfy many people.

In Thailand—particularly in the North and Northeast regions of the country, where the technique seems to be most popular and is commonly applied in drinking foods—the fermentation is accomplished by leaving the meat out in the hot, relatively dry local climes until it has sufficiently soured. Unless you live in, say, Hawaii, Florida, LA, or Arizona, you might need to be creative about re-creating the proper environmental conditions.

Your task is to find a way to keep the meat in a warm, dry space. Ideally, you'd ferment at a relatively consistent temperature that falls within the range that encourages fermentation: about 95°F to 100°F / 35°C to 38°C. Achieving these conditions might mean keeping the meat outside, or on top of your fridge where the rising dry heat from the coils makes for an environment slightly warmer than room temperature. Maybe you have an oven with a pilot light or a bread-proofing setting, or you own a proofing box or a space heater. Use your Yankee ingenuity.

Depending on conditions, it will take up to two days for the meat to ferment. If the temperature is lower, fermentation will happen more slowly; if higher, more quickly. The ultimate level of sourness is up to you. Sniff or, depending on your squeamishness, taste the meat to assess its progress. (If for some reason it doesn't smell sour after the advised

◊ ◊ ◊

A deep-fry thermometer

A large spider skimmer
(recommended)

Pork Ribs

420 g / 2¼ cups freshly
cooked Khao Niaw
(Sticky rice), page 248

4 pounds / 1.8 kg pork
baby back ribs, cut
crosswise through the
bone into racks 2 inches /
5 cm long (Asian butchers
sell them already cut)

52 g / ¼ cup Tusino-style
curing powder (such as
Lee or Por Kwan brand)

52 g / 3 tablespoons plus
2½ teaspoons Morton
Tender Quick meat
curing salt

140 g / scant 1 cup peeled
garlic cloves

Neutral oil (such as soybean
or palm), for deep-frying
(about 12 cups / 2.8 L)

To Serve Alongside

White cabbage wedges

Unsalted roasted peanuts

Peeled fresh ginger,
cut into small pieces

Fresh Thai chiles

---

time, don't wait any longer.) This should go without saying, but if it turns black or smells rotten, don't eat it.

For practical, and perhaps legal reasons, I should warn that although this is the method employed by the Thai operations I've observed, it would not meet the rigorous standards set out by various regulatory outfits in charge of policing the way food in American restaurants is made. That said, Thais do it every day and they're still here. I've done it, and I'm still here. But, yes, proceed at your own peril.

Ferment the pork ribs

Rinse the rice in a bowl of room-temperature tap water to cool it down, breaking up clumps, then drain very well.

Cut the pork racks into individual riblets, pat them dry with paper towels, and put them in a large bowl.

Combine the curing powder and curing salt in a small bowl and stir well. Add the garlic to a food processor and process until minced. Add the rice to the processor and process until broken down and well combined but not pureed. Sprinkle the curing mixture over the ribs, then, using your hands, toss and rub the mixture on the ribs to distribute it evenly. Add the rice mixture and again toss and rub to distribute it evenly.

Divide the ribs evenly among a few large, resealable bags. They should be crowded in the bags, not in a single layer, and surrounded by the rice mixture. Seal the bags, forcing out as much air as possible. Place the bags on a large sheet pan and leave the pan in a warm (90°F to 100°F / 32°C to 38°C), dry place, flipping the bags twice a day, until the meat has achieved the sourness you prefer. This will take up to 2 days, depending on the ambient temperature and your preference. Open the bags and sniff the meat to assess its progress. At this point, the ribs can be stored in their bags in the fridge for up to 3 days before continuing.

Fry and serve the ribs

Select a heavy pot at least 12 inches / 30 cm wide and pour in the oil to a depth of about 3 inches / 7.5 cm. Set the pot over high heat and heat the oil to 325°F / 165°C. Use the thermometer to test the temperature, measuring the oil at the center of the vessel and carefully stirring the oil occasionally to ensure a consistent temperature. Line a large sheet pan with paper towels or newspaper and set it near the stove.

While the oil is heating, rinse the ribs and pat them dry. Fry the ribs in four batches to avoid crowding the oil. Carefully add the first batch to the hot oil and fry the ribs until the outsides are a ruddy golden brown, about 3 minutes. Using the spider or a slotted spoon, transfer the ribs to the prepared pan to drain. Repeat with the remaining ribs.

Serve the ribs with the cabbage, peanuts, ginger, and chiles for eating between bites.

MUU YAANG THAWT

Fried grilled pork   หมูย่างทอด

Charoen Suan Aek is hard to find but easy to love. The restaurant is in Chiang Mai, down a winding street that takes you into what looks to be a purely residential enclave. Then you spot the dozen or so tables under a corrugated steel roof. Here you'll find some of the best *aahaan meuang* (the food of the North) in the country.

Since I shamefully don't read Thai, I rely on friends to read the menu aloud, so I can get a sense of what's on offer. On my first visit, my girlfriend, Kung, did the honors. When I heard her say, *"Muu yaang thawt"* I did a double take. I've eaten about a thousand kilos of *muu yaang* (grilled pork) in my time. I've eaten almost as much *muu thawt* (fried pork). I must've misheard, so I asked Kung which of the two she meant. No, she explained, I'd heard right: the dish was pork that was first slowly grilled over smoldering charcoal, picking up plenty of smoky flavor in the process, then immersed in hot fat, giving the exterior a welcome crispness. Predictably, it was extremely delicious. I haven't spotted the dish outside Charoen Suan Aek, though it might be common enough for all I know. What I do know is that if anything goes better with rice whiskey or beer, I haven't found it. ◊ ***serves 4 to 6***

◊ ◊ ◊

A grill, preferably charcoal (highly recommended), grate oiled

A deep-fry thermometer

A large spider skimmer (recommended)

Pork and Marinade

1 tablespoon Thai fish sauce

1 tablespoon Thai seasoning sauce (look for the green cap)

8 g / 2 teaspoons MSG (optional but highly recommended)

Freshly ground black pepper

1 (18-ounce / 500-g) piece boneless skin-on pork leg

To Finish

Neutral oil (such as soybean or palm), for deep-frying (about 12 cups / 2.8 L)

1 (5⅓-ounce / 150-g) piece package tempura batter mix, preferably Gogi brand

½ cup / 120 ml Jaew (Isaan dipping sauce), page 245

Marinate the pork

Mix together the fish sauce, seasoning sauce, MSG, and pepper to taste in a large bowl until the MSG fully dissolves.

Cut the pork against the grain of the muscle into pieces about 6 inches / 15 cm long, 2½ inches / 6 cm wide, and 1 inch / 2.5 cm thick. Do not discard the fat—it's the best part. Add the pork to the bowl with the marinade and use your hands to mix and massage the pork. Cover and marinate in the fridge for at least 2 hours or up to 8 hours.

Grill the pork

Prepare the grill to cook with medium heat (see page 129). Set a large cooling rack on a sheet pan.

Put the pork on the grill grate and cook, turning it occasionally, until it turns a pleasant reddish brown and the skin puffs slightly, about 30 minutes. (The pork will be cooked through sooner, but the long, slow grilling adds flavor.) Transfer the pork to the rack to let any juices drip off, and let it cool to the touch.

Fry and serve the pork

Select a heavy pot at least 12 inches / 30 cm wide and pour in the oil to a depth of 2 to 3 inches / 5 to 7.5 cm. Set the pot over high heat and bring the oil to 300°F / 150°C. Use the thermometer to test the temperature, measuring the oil at the center of the vessel and carefully stirring the oil occasionally to ensure a consistent temperature. Line a large sheet pan with paper towels or newspaper and set it near the stove. Put the tempura batter mix in a wide, shallow bowl.

Cook the pork in small batches to avoid crowding the oil: Add a few pieces of the pork to the batter mix and toss briefly to coat them with a very thin layer. Remove the pieces from the bowl, shaking off any excess mix, and carefully add them to the hot oil. Fry the pieces, turning them occasionally, until deep golden brown, 2 to 3 minutes. Using the spider or a slotted spoon, transfer the pork to the prepared pan to drain. Repeat with the remaining pork.

Slice the pork crosswise into bite-size pieces and serve right away with the dipping sauce.

MAM

Isaan beef and liver sausage ##### หมํ่า

Once upon a time, *mam* was the sausage that got away. I spotted it for the first time a few years back, when I took a road trip from Chiang Mai to Vientiane, the capital of Laos. Our route took my associates and me through Isaan, the Northeastern region of Thailand, which shares a border—not to mention cultural and culinary identity—with Laos. As we drove through a rural town, I saw a roadside vendor holding a stick hung with links of dark, ruddy brown sausage. I figured it must be *mam*, one of those Isaan specialties I'd heard tales of but that wasn't easy to find at the Isaan restaurants that outside the region itself. And even if it wasn't *mam*, I'd buy it anyway. I've never met a sausage that didn't deserve appraisal. I purchased some, stashed it in the trunk, and to my dismay, forgot about it until we'd finished the long, hot journey to Laos. With a heavy heart, I tossed it.

Only recently did I make it back to Isaan with enough time for *mam* scouting. (That's one problem with traveling to the Northeast—so many dishes make the docket.) With a little advice, I wound up at the restaurant Khrua Isaan, in the city of Khon Kaen, where proprietor Mae Phranom makes and serves several local sausages. I didn't have to ask what was on offer—the evidence was draped on virtually every surface, including a straw tray on the seat of a motorcycle, in various states of cured. There was *sai krawk*, one type made with pork and another with beef, and there was the elusive *mam*.

When I arrived, Mae Phranom was at work, chopping meat on a wooden block. Nearby, a cauldron of *tom saep* bubbled away, a rendition especially heavy on the aromatics and organs. She generously fielded my *mam* questions, gruffly outlining the dish and letting me watch

◊ ◊ ◊

Khawng Thawt: Fried Foods

as she fed lean beef and liver into a grinder, seasoned the mixture with salt, MSG, garlic, and chile, and filled casings to form fat links. She then set them to cure, hanging them in partial sun for several days so they firmed up and took on a slight tang from fermentation.

We ordered what in the States might have been advertised as a "sampling of artisan sausage" and got to taste her merchandise, the three varieties of cased meat deep fried and hacked into rough, crumbly chunks and served with whole chiles, raw garlic cloves, and fiery *jaew* spiked, in the local fashion, with remarkably bitter *dii* (cow bile). The *mam* was drier, leaner, and less sour than the more familiar *sai krawk*, rich and minerally like blood sausage, salty, and just slightly spicy. It shared the intensity of flavor, though not the flavor profile, of salami rather than, say, the mild meatiness of bratwurst—in other words, this is not a link you'd take down all by yourself. With plenty of drinks, just a couple could feed a crowd.

Despite my crash course, I'm still unclear whether the name *mam* (which means "spleen") refers to an occasional ingredient (there was no spleen in Mae Phranom's version, but certainly there might be in others) or the look of the links (I've never seen that particular organ up close but a cursory Google search suggests a vague resemblance both in shape and color). Not even my culinary betters seem to have an answer. I can tell you, though, that you can make a fine approximation of the sausage outside of Isaan. If you're up for it, you can even reasonably replicate Mae Phranom's *jaew*, following the recipe on page 245 and adding a dash or two of bile, which I've spotted in small bottles in markets with a Lao focus.

◊ *makes about 3 pounds / 1360 g; about 9 (6-inch / 15-cm) links*

◊ ◊ ◊

A meat grinder and a
¼-inch / 6-mm die

A sausage maker or
sausage-stuffer funnel

Kitchen twine, cut into
9 (3-inch / 7.5-cm) lengths

A deep-fry thermometer

Sausages

150 g / ¾ cup freshly
cooked Khao Niaw (Sticky
rice), page 248, or Khao
Hom Mali (Jasmine rice),
page 247

28 ounces / 800 g boneless
beef loin, top round, or
other very lean cut, cut into
1-inch / 2.5-cm chunks

9 ounces / 250 g beef liver,
cut into 1-inch / 2.5-cm
chunks

60 g / ⅓ cup finely
chopped garlic

20 g / 4 teaspoons iodized
table salt

16 g / 4 teaspoons
MSG (optional but
recommended)

4 g / 4 teaspoons Phrik
Pon Khua (Toasted-chile
powder), page 233

About 8 feet / 2.4 m
natural hog or beef middle
sausage casings, thawed if
frozen or soaked in water
for 5 minutes if salted

Neutral oil (such as
soybean or palm), for
deep-frying (about
12 cups / 2.8 L)

To Serve Alongside

Green cabbage wedges

Unsalted roasted peanuts

Peeled fresh ginger, thinly
sliced against the grain

Fresh Thai chiles

Jaew (Isaan dipping sauce),
page 245

Make the sausages

Rinse the rice in a bowl of room-temperature tap water to cool it down, breaking up clumps, then drain very well.

Put the beef loin and liver on a plate and chill, uncovered, in the freezer until the edges have frozen, 30 to 45 minutes. Briefly freezing the meat will make it easier to grind and prevent it from emulsifying.

When the meat is chilled, fit the meat grinder with the die and run the beef and the liver through the grinder once. Put the ground meat in a large bowl.

Rinse the rice in a bowl of room-temperature water to cool it down, breaking up the clumps into individual grains, then drain well. Add the cooled rice, garlic, salt, MSG, and chile powder to the ground meat and mix with your hands until well combined.

Rinse the casings well under running cold water, then rinse the insides by putting one end of each casing around the mouth of a faucet and letting the water run through it for a few minutes. This will also show you whether the casing is broken. Use about 5 feet / 1.5 m of unbroken casings for your sausage (a continuous length of 5 feet / 1.5 m, however, isn't necessary). Discard any broken casing—that's why you bought so much.

If you have a sausage maker, good for you. If not, you can stuff the casings with the help of a sausage-stuffer funnel or regular funnel. First, insert the narrow end of the funnel into the open end of the casing. Next, tie a tight knot at the other end of the casing, and then gather as much of the casing as you can onto the funnel. Push the meat, a few tablespoons at a time, through the funnel and into the casing. Whenever you have a good 6 inches / 15 cm or so of meat in the casing, stop for a moment, hold the open end of the casing with one hand, and use the other hand to gently but firmly force the meat toward the knotted end. It's ideal to slightly overstuff the casings here. Before you twist the sausage into links, you want to make sure you have a good 8 inches / 15 cm or so of empty casing left at the open end.

Using a toothpick or thin wooden skewer, prick the casing near any air bubbles you spot. Then slowly run one hand along the sausage from opening end to the knotted end to ensure the meat is as evenly distributed as possible and to eliminate any remaining air pockets. Use a knife tip to prick the casing about every 1 inch / 2.5 cm so the sausage won't burst when you cook it.

Starting at the tied end of the casing, twist the sausage into 6-inch / 15-cm links. Each time you twist, tie a piece of the kitchen twine around the twist to secure it. Wipe the outsides of the sausages with a damp towel, then dry them.

Ferment the sausages

Hang the links and ferment according to the directions on page 110 until the meat has achieved the sourness you prefer. This will take up to 3 days, depending on the ambient temperature and your preference. When the sausages are ready, they'll be firm, dark, and dry to the touch and will smell slightly sour.

At this point, you can wrap the links in plastic wrap and store them in the refrigerator for up to 5 days, or put them in freezer bags and freeze them for up to 3 months. Before cooking, cut between each link to separate them.

Cook and serve the sausages

Select a heavy pot at least 12 inches / 30 cm wide and pour in the oil to a depth of 2 to 3 inches / 5 to 7.5 cm. Set the pot over high heat and heat the oil to 325°F to 350°F / 165°C to 180°C. Use the thermometer to test the temperature, measuring the oil at the center of the vessel and carefully stirring the oil occasionally to ensure a consistent temperature. Line a large sheet pan with paper towels or newspaper and set it near the stove.

Fry the sausages in batches of three until crispy on the outside and hot on the inside, 2 to 3 minutes. Using tongs, transfer them to the prepared pan to drain.

Slice the sausages into bite-size pieces and arrange on a plate. Serve right away with the cabbage, peanuts, ginger, and chiles for eating between bites of sausage and with the *jaew* in a bowl for dipping.

121

Pork ribs cooked "underwater," a dish with a tricky name and an unusual cooking technique.

SII KHRONG MUU TAI NAAM

ซี่โครงหมูใต้น้ำ   Pork ribs cooked "underwater"

SPECIAL EQUIPMENT

A Thai granite mortar and pestle

An 11- to 12-inch / 28- to 30-cm round, heavy pot

A heatproof mixing bowl, big enough to rise above the lip of the pot and form an airtight seal against the rim

When I set out to write this book, my goal was to both report on my favorite versions of *aahaan kap klaem* and learn about a few I'd never had. To that end, I chatted up friends and vendors, chefs and beer barons, then spent a troubling number of late nights following leads down alleyways in Bangkok, into dirt lots scattered with tables up North, and sausage factories in Isaan. Yet this dish came to me in Slovenia of all places. On a detour to catch a leg of the farewell tour of my pals' band, I met up with the great chef David Thompson and his colleague Part. Over Slovenian sausage in Ljubljana, Part turned me onto an Isaan dish called *pik kai tai naam* (chicken wings cooked "underwater").

Its unusual method caught my eye—after the chicken is marinated, it's cooked in a pot topped with a bowl of ice water, whose sides seal the pot. (Get it, "underwater"?) As the meat cooks, it releases its juices, yet instead of ultimately escaping as steam, they hit the cold bowl, condense, and drip back down. The same principle is at work in the distillation of *lao khao*, where big woks filled with cool water rest on the opening of vats of simmering fermented-rice liquid. The setup strikes me as so similar, in fact, that I wouldn't be surprised if the dish's technique had been devised by someone sitting around observing a *lao khao* operation. No matter the origin, I'll tell you this: deliciousness ensues.

After plenty of discussion and some heavy Googling in Thai, I was ready to try it out. Once I got back to my lair, I gave it a shot, using pork ribs instead of chicken wings and fashioning a paste from fresh turmeric, galangal, lemongrass, and both fresh and dried chiles. And while I'll admit to missing the mark on practically every first crack I take at an unfamiliar dish, this one was a rip-roaring success. After cooking in their own fat and juices, the ribs are tender with a pleasant chew. All it needs is sticky rice and your tipple of choice. ◊ *serves 6 to 8*

Make the paste

Combine the dried chiles and salt in the mortar and pound firmly, scraping and stirring with a spoon occasionally, until you have a fairly fine powder, about 3 minutes. Add the lemongrass and pound, occasionally stopping to scrape down the sides of the mortar, until you have a fairly smooth, slightly fibrous paste, about 2 minutes. Add the galangal, turmeric, and cilantro roots and do the same. Add the garlic and do the same. Finally, add the fresh chiles and do the same.

You'll have about 75 g / ¼ cup paste. You can use it right away, or you can store it in an airtight container in the fridge for up to 1 week or in the freezer for up to 6 months.

Cook the pork ribs

Cut the pork racks into individual riblets. Combine the ribs, paste, lime leaves, fish sauce, sugar, and MSG in a large bowl and mix well with your hands, firmly rubbing the seasonings onto the ribs.

Heat the oil in the heavy pot over medium-high heat just until it begins to smoke. Add the ribs in a single layer and cook until lightly browned on one side, about 5 minutes. Flip the ribs, lower the heat to medium-low, and set the heatproof bowl into the pot, creating an airtight seal. Fill the bowl with ice, then pour water into the bowl until the water level is just above the rim of the pot.

Cook, stirring the ice mixture occasionally, until the ribs are tender with a nice chew, 30 to 35 minutes. This is important: keep the water in the bowl cold. Whenever the ice is nearly melted, quickly but carefully empty the bowl, return the bowl to the pot, and refill it with ice and water.

Transfer the ribs along with any juices to a platter, sprinkle with the green onions, sawtooth herb, and cilantro, and serve right away.

Paste

5 g stemmed dried Thai chiles

3 g kosher salt

15 g thinly sliced lemongrass (tender parts only), from about 2 large stalks

8 g peeled fresh or thawed frozen galangal, thinly sliced against the grain

2 g peeled fresh or thawed frozen yellow turmeric, thinly sliced against the grain

2 g cilantro roots

20 g peeled garlic cloves, halved lengthwise

20 g stemmed fresh red or green Thai chiles

Pork ribs

2¼ pounds / 1 kg pork baby back ribs, cut crosswise through the bone into racks 2 inches / 5 cm wide, then into individual ribs

3 g / 1 tablespoon very thinly sliced fresh or frozen makrut lime leaves (stems removed if thick)

2 teaspoons Thai fish sauce

4 g / 1 teaspoon granulated sugar

2 g / ½ teaspoon MSG (optional but highly recommended)

2 tablespoons neutral oil (such as rice bran or canola)

1 (10-pound / 4.5 kg) bag ice

10 g / 2 tablespoons sliced (¼ inch / 6 mm) green onions

4 g / 2 tablespoons thinly sliced sawtooth herb

4 g / 2 tablespoons coarsely chopped cilantro (thin stems and leaves)

KHAWNG YAANG

GRILLED FOODS

ของย่าง

A NOTE ON THAI GRILLING

Grilling the Thai way is essential for executing a significant portion of the food in this book. It also offers a few valuable lessons for home cooks even if they don't make any of the book's recipes.

Thai cooks grill in so many ways that a general technique seems to defy definition. I've seen an infinite number of setups, from an enameled metal tray filled with charcoal and topped with a precariously balanced grate to repurposed oil drums to more sophisticated contraptions. At SP Chicken, for instance, my grilled-chicken guru Mr. Lit, modified a rotisserie rig to his specs, and today his pint-size birds cook on vertical spits, rotating beside a wall of hot coals.

Yet two near constants exist that ultimately distinguish the Thai way of grilling. The first is charcoal. Nowadays, you'll find plenty of gas grills at homes and restaurants in Thailand. But without the flavor and aroma contributed by smoldering coals, the food you cook will be lacking. The second is the degree of heat to which ingredients are subjected, which counts as the clearest place of divergence from the Western approach.

Think of the typical brute-force American way to cook steak. In back-yards from Portland to Brooklyn, rib eyes spit and sizzle on grill grates just a few inches from cherry-red coals. I've seen this brutalize-both-sides technique fail much more than it succeeds. But the goal always seems to be a juicy, pink center and a well-branded exterior, the lines of char like desperate proof that the meat was cooked outdoors.

In Thailand, I've seen a wide range of heat applied to protein. Sure, a few dishes require relatively high temperatures, but many more rely on gentler cooking or even on heat so low that the technique probably qualifies as hot smoking. Rarely if ever do cooks apply the sort of intense heat you see back home. Not only does the temperature tend toward the lower end of the spectrum, but the intended result is different, too. Medium rare is almost unheard of in Thailand. Meat, with few exceptions, is cooked completely through (or served completely raw). The moderate heat—somewhere in between the conductive heat required to brown and the radiant heat needed to bake—allows the meat to enjoy the full benefit of the charcoal, picking up its smoky flavor, cooking all the way through, and developing a crust, not char.

In fact, anything that approaches black tends to be fastidiously snipped off. I haven't adopted this habit, which is probably linked to a fear of the carcinogens supposedly created by high-heat cooking over a fire. But I do embrace the Thai technique, and not only out of loyalty to tradition. In recent years, science-minded food writers have demonstrated that judicious heat makes for better flavor, and that those grill marks are more about looks than taste. They've also disproven the stubborn brown-before-you-braise gospel. That makes at least two ways Thai cooks have long been ahead of the culinary curve.

GRILLING AT HOME

The recipes in this book require three general levels of heat: low, medium, and relatively hot. What follows is my take on how to achieve them. Each recipe that requires grilling will note the correct level of heat, the intended appearance of the result, and the approximate grilling time. You might have your own method and preferences. You might even decide to use a gas grill, in which case you can ignore my sermon on regulating temperature and just turn the dial. I don't recommend it, but it's your prerogative, Bobby Brown.

Getting started: Thai-style grilling at home begins the same way all grilling should. First, you ignite the charcoal (a chimney starter is the easiest way, but the method is up to you) and let it burn until the coals are no longer smoking and have turned gray. Dump the coals into the grill, spread them into an even layer, and add the grill grate. Let the grate get hot, then scrub it clean with a grill brush. Use long tongs to grab an oil-dampened rag and rub it onto the grate so your food won't stick.

Cooking: To achieve and maintain a particular grilling temperature, some people focus on controlling the fire. They vary the type of charcoal. They open and close vents to stoke or starve it. They add more coals to increase the heat. Aside from recommending charcoal—I typically choose long-burning lump, ideally coconut charcoal or Japanese *binchōtan*, over briquettes, which burn quickly and give off a chemical odor—I say focus less on the heat source itself and more on the distance you put between food and the heat source.

I've watched Khun Wut, the grill master at Paa Daeng Jin Tup, just outside Chiang Mai, operate a rudimentary pulley system to raise and lower racks full of MSG-marinated flank steak, banana leaf–wrapped pig brains, and pork teat. I've watched Mr. Lit lean impaled chickens toward the glowing coals when they need color and away when they're getting too dark. I've seen chef friends splurge on shiny modern grills that feature a crank to move the grate up and down. There's a reason profes-sional cooks of all stripes use distance this way. Charcoal fire responds slowly to attempts to adjust heat. Smoldering coals take time to cool. New coals take time to ignite and ash over. But the moment you move meat farther from or closer to hot coals, you've changed the temperature at which food is cooking. Choosing distance as your variable means you can worry less about the idiosyncrasies of your charcoal or grill and unpredictable concerns like the goddamn weather.

My suggestion is to get a grill with an adjustable grate (they're not always expensive), or find a simple way to adjust the height of what you have, like making a platform with a couple of aluminum foil–wrapped bricks. Frequently flipping can serve a similar purpose—basically keeping meat from charring.

So for the recipes in this book, know that you can achieve the proper heat with any intensity of fire. Cooking farther from blazing coals can have the same effect as cooking close to temperate ones.

SAVE YOUR ASH

Frequent grillers will find themselves with plenty of ash. I used to dump mine, but not anymore. Now I do what I've seen so many vendors in Thailand do: employ the powdery remains of charcoal to control their fires. Sprinkling a light blanket of ash, often dampened with water, on hot charcoal before you start cooking evens out the heat and keeps charcoal burning longer by moderating oxygen flow. You can also use it to quell flare-ups. So every time after you grill, save your ash. Make sure it's fully extinguished, then transfer it to a metal bucket.

At Paa Daeng Jin Tup, Luung Wut smashes beef with a sledgehammer on a chopping block made from a tamarind tree.

Jin tup, properly pounded to shreds, the classic beef (left) and an equally compelling pork version (right).

JIN TUP

Hammered flank steak จิ้นตุ๊บ

If you frequent enough Northern countryside hangouts where the booze flows freely, you'll probably hear this dish being made—*wham, wham, wham*—even before you spot it. You'll look over at a guy standing at a fat wooden chopping block, whacking beef with a hammer until it shreds. I like this sound. It means there's good food ahead.

Jin means "meat" in Northern Thai dialect (it's *neua* in Central speak). *Tup* essentially means "smash" and that's what cooks do, striking the meat with a hammer after it's been slowly grilled to well-done. No pink-centered medium rare here. Order *jin tup* and a small plate containing chewy snarls of flesh, slightly smoky from charcoal and amped up from *phong chu roht* (good old-fashioned MSG), will show up on your table. If your waiter is kind or you have a clued-in friend, you'll also get *naam phrik khaa* in the form of a coarse dry powder or a murky liquid—or both. The former is a paste of chiles, lemongrass, garlic, and galangal painstakingly cooked in a wok until any moisture has evaporated. The latter is this parched version rehydrated with tart-sweet tamarind water. Either way, this stuff is to *jin tup* what ketchup is to fries. ◊ *serves 8 to 10*

◊ ◊ ◊

A grill, preferably charcoal (highly recommended), grate oiled

A solid wooden chopping block (recommended)

A clean engineer's (ball-peen) hammer or other roughly 2-pound / 900-g sledgehammer

———

6 cups / 1.4 L warm tap water

50 g / ⅓ cup kosher salt

50 g / ¼ cup granulated sugar

25 g / 2 tablespoons MSG

3 g / 1 teaspoon black peppercorns

35 g / ¼ cup thinly sliced (⅛ inch / 3 mm) peeled fresh or thawed frozen galangal

24 g / 8 unpeeled garlic cloves

30 g / 30 cilantro roots

2 large stalks lemongrass, bottom 1 inch / 2.5 cm, top 9 inches / 23 cm and outer layer removed

2½ pounds / 1.2 kg flank steak, silver skin removed, fat left on

Naam Phrik Khaa (Galangal chile dip), page 67, for serving

Marinate the steak

Combine the water, salt, sugar, MSG, and peppercorns in a tall, narrow container and stir well to dissolve the salt, sugar, and MSG. Lightly smash the galangal with a pestle, a pan, or the flat surface of a knife blade to release the oils. Do the same to the garlic, cilantro roots, and lemongrass. Chop the lemongrass into about 1-inch / 2.5-cm pieces. Add the galangal, garlic, cilantro roots, and lemongrass to the container and stir.

Butterfly any part of the flank steak that is thicker than ¾ inch / 2 cm. Prick the steak all over with a fork (this helps the marinade penetrate the meat). Cut the steak into pieces about 3 by 6 inches / 7.5 by 15 cm, with the grain of the meat running the long way. Transfer the steak to the container, making sure it is submerged. Cover and refrigerate for at least 4 hours or up to 1 day.

Grill the steak

Prepare a grill to cook with medium heat (see page 129). Let the steak come to room temperature. Remove the steak pieces from the marinade and discard the marinade. Put the pieces on the grill grate and grill, flipping them occasionally, until they are lightly browned (you're not looking for any char) and fully cooked with no pink remaining inside, about 30 minutes. Precise doneness is not important here.

Transfer the steak to the chopping block or a cutting board with a towel underneath and whack the pieces with the hammer until they break into a web of fine shreds but not into pieces. Roughly chop into bite-size pieces and serve right away with the chile dip.

BBQ

Thai-style barbecue beef skewers บาร์บีคิว

Like most travelers to Bangkok, I took refuge—if you can call it that—in Sukhumvit.

Long ago, for several years running, I would fly into Bangkok late and head straight to the stretch of Sukhumvit Road that served as the center of *farang* nightlife, featuring activities both legitimate and not. Besides a bustling night market, there were what seemed to be a million bars, and, most important to me at the time, plenty of dirt-cheap, pretty nice hotels with names like Loft 23. Twenty bucks got you a room at a shiny place that looked as if it had been built the day before you got there. Sukhumvit served as a place of comfort and spectacle, and you didn't have to speak Thai to get along. The landscape, grimy and hectic, is familiar in the way it matches the tourist's idea of what Bangkok is supposed to be.

A spot at one of the street-side bars afforded me a solid view of the action from a safe distance. The sidewalks were (and still are) a parade of blotto foreigners and taxi drivers, transvestites and Thai women in hijabs (the city's Muslim population has an enclave there), bums and prostitutes and hustlers, who for some reason left you more or less alone if you had a seat and a cold one. A beer or three also helped knock me out, which was necessary since I typically arrived after midnight and my body, still on Pacific Standard Time, thought it was time for lunch.

Three trips in a row, I wound up at the same perch, talking with the same vendor. He operated a bike-powered cart with a grill attached and had a deal with a bar's owner, who let him sell to patrons. The first time I saw him, I asked him what he had. "Barbecue," he said, motioning toward skewers of beef, chile, and pineapple.

◊ ◊ ◊

Khawng Yaang: Grilled Foods

12 wooden skewers, each about 8 inches / 20 cm long, soaked in tepid water for 30 minutes

A grill, preferably charcoal (highly recommended), grate oiled

A food-safe brush

---

1 pound (455 g) boneless beef chuck flap or flank steak

12 pieces peeled pineapple, each 1 inch / 2.5 cm long, 1 inch / 2.5 cm wide, and ¼ inch / 6 mm thick (about 4 ounces / 115 g)

12 pieces seeded, deveined bell pepper or jalapeño chile, each 1 inch / 2.5 cm long by 1 inch / 2.5 cm wide (about 3 ounces / 85 g)

3 tablespoons Thai sweet soy sauce

3 tablespoons Thai fish sauce

I was hungry, so I ordered a couple, then a couple more, chatting until the scene on the street had gone from entertaining to weird, and I was finally ready to pass out.

Since I'd had my first barbecue experience on Sukhumvit, I figured the dish was exclusively honky fare. But spotting the skewers at a *muay thai* fight outside a rural police station an hour from Chiang Mai, as well as in other places where I was the only white guy for miles, suggested a different conclusion. My theory is that they're an example of Western food made Thai, not the more familiar other way around. Brushed with an intense two-ingredient mixture of fish sauce and sweet soy sauce and barbecued (in the grilling sense of the word), no one would mistake this for the beef skewers you find in back-yards from Teaneck, New Jersey, to Portland, Oregon. It's damn good stuff, though. ◊ *serves 4 to 6*

Using a sharp knife, cut the beef against the grain into strips about 2 inches / 5 cm long, 1 inch / 2.5 cm wide, and ⅛ inch / 3 mm thick.

Thread 1 pineapple piece and then 1 pepper piece onto each skewer. Push them both toward the bottom of the skewer, leaving about 2 inches / 5 cm empty at the end to hold on to. Thread 5 or 6 beef strips onto each skewer, bunching them together and making sure the tip of the skewer isn't exposed (otherwise it will burn). Push the pineapple and pepper toward the tip end of the skewer until the pepper touches the beef.

Prepare the grill to cook with medium-high heat (see page 129).

Combine the soy sauce and fish sauce in a small bowl and stir well. Generously brush each skewer all over with the mixture. Put the skewers on the grill grate and grill, turning them frequently, until the beef is cooked to medium well, about 8 minutes.

Transfer to a plate and serve right away.

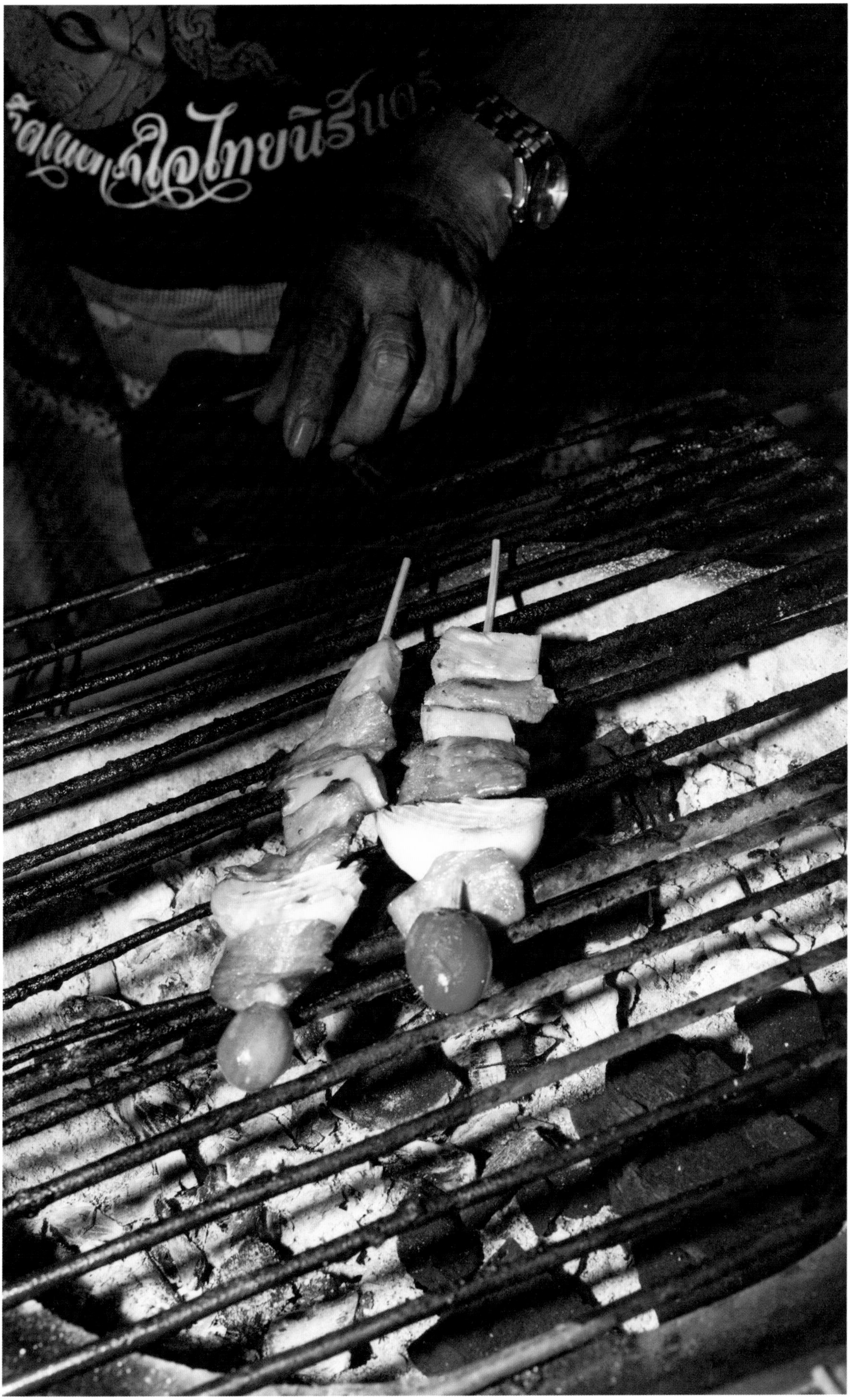

AEP SAMOENG MUU

Pig's brains grilled in banana leaf   แอ็บสมองหมู

I first had this Northern Thai dish at a restaurant tucked behind a hostel in Chiang Mai's tourist ghetto. At the time, I was still staying in *farang*-friendly places, in this case at a nearby guesthouse. But whenever I got hungry, I went in search of the opposite.

Despite its location, this particular restaurant was not geared toward tourists. The place was in the "shop house" style of Thai eateries: half living space, half restaurant. Several generations of family members probably lived upstairs, cooked, prepped, and lounged around back. There were a few tables, but they were piled with a week's worth of newspapers or taken up by a little kid playing with an action figure. Most customers pulled up on motorcycles and left soon after, carrying plastic bags filled with various shapes of banana leaf–wrapped parcels that had been slowly cooking over charcoal on the grill out front.

An English menu listed a few things the owner thought tourists might want. The rest of the menu was in Thai, which even today I still can't read. But I spoke rudimentary Thai, so I walked up to the older guy manning the grill and started asking questions. He ticked off what he had going, and I caught the word *samoeng* or "brain." I'll have that, I told him, partly because I was curious and partly in an

◊ ◊ ◊

          Khawng Yaang: Grilled Foods

A Thai granite mortar and pestle

2 wooden skewers, broken into about 5-inch / 12-cm pieces, soaked in tepid water for 30 minutes

A grill, preferably charcoal (highly recommended), grate oiled

———

Paste

7 g stemmed dried Mexican puya chiles

3 g kosher salt

35 g thinly sliced lemongrass (tender parts only) from about 5 large stalks

35 g peeled fresh or thawed frozen galangal, thinly sliced against the grain

35 g peeled fresh or thawed frozen yellow turmeric root, thinly sliced against the grain

45 g peeled garlic cloves, halved lengthwise

45 g peeled Asian shallots, thinly sliced against the grain

9 g Kapi Kung (Homemade shrimp paste), page 238

attempt to show him that I was, unlike many foreigners who stayed nearby, an open, adventurous eater. I doubt he was impressed.

Chatting with the man behind the grill, I learned that the majority of the Thai menu was composed of Isaan dishes, fare from the Northeastern region of the country. But the man himself was from Northern Thailand, of which Chiang Mai is the de facto capital. That explained the *aep samoeng muu*, which I'd later learn was a staple of Northern Thai countryside drinking establishments. Essentially, it is pig's brains scrunched by hand (*kluk,* as the method is known) with curry paste, packed in banana leaf, and grilled. He was selling the dish and its banana-wrapped brethren in the way a Mexican guy running a deli in New York might offer a taco or two along with his roster of turkey and roast beef sandwiches.

I took a few parcels back to a table, unfolded the one with brain, and after a good swig of beer, dug in. The texture was custardy, a bit like scrambled eggs but richer, and the fragrance and flavor complex from a heady paste of chile, lemongrass, galangal, turmeric root, and the perfume of lime leaf. The dish has become a favorite of mine, something I order whenever it's on offer.

◊ *serves 4 to 8*

Make the paste

Combine the chiles and salt in the mortar and pound firmly, occasionally stopping to scrape down the sides of the mortar and stirring with a spoon after about 3 minutes, until you have a fairly fine powder (some larger flecks are fine), about 5 minutes. Add the lemongrass and pound, again occasionally stopping to scrape down the sides of the mortar, until you have a fairly smooth, slightly fibrous paste, about 2 minutes. Do the same with the galangal, then the turmeric, then the garlic, and then the shallots, fully pounding each ingredient before moving on to the next. Finally, pound in the shrimp paste until fully incorporated, about 1 minute.

You'll have about 210 g / ¾ cup paste. Set aside 70 g / ¼ cup for this recipe and store the remainder in an airtight container in the fridge for up to 1 week or in the freezer for up to 6 months.

Season and wrap the pig's brains

Rinse the brains well under cold running water, drain well, and pat dry. Combine the brains, cilantro, green onions, lime leaves, salt, a few grinds of pepper, and the reserved paste in a bowl. Use your hands to squeeze and scrunch the ingredients together to distribute them well, about 1 minute. The delicate brains will turn to mush.

Trim any stems from the banana leaf pieces. Pass both sides of each piece very briefly over a gas flame to make them more pliable and less likely to break when you fold them. Put a piece of banana leaf, shiny side down and with the ridges running toward you, on a work surface. Put a second piece, shiny side up and with the ridges perpendicular to the ridges on the first piece, on top. This will make your packets stronger. Put half of the brain mixture on the center.

Now you're going to make a neat, compact square packet. Starting with the edge closest to you, fold both layers of banana leaf over the brain mixture to enclose it. Next, fold over the edge farthest from you. Fold the short edges over each other to create a tidy packet. Use a piece of skewer to stitch together the leaf pieces you just folded so the packet stays closed. Be careful not to puncture the part of the packet that contains the brain. Repeat with the remaining leaf pieces, brain mixture, and skewers.

Grill the pig's brains

Prepare the grill to cook with medium-low heat (see page 129). Put the packets, seam side up, on the grill grate and cook, carefully turning them over every 5 minutes, until they are slightly charred on both sides and the brain mixture is firm to the touch when you press your fingers against the banana leaf, 20 to 30 minutes. If the packets start to char after only 5 minutes, the heat is too high. Keep in mind that brains are relatively forgiving, and you're not shooting for precise doneness.

Serve right away, letting people open the packages themselves.

Pig's Brains

1 pound / 455 g fresh or thawed frozen pig's brains

8 g / ¼ cup coarsely chopped cilantro (thin stems and leaves)

20 g / ¼ cup sliced (¼ inch / 6 mm) green onions

9 g / 3 tablespoons very thinly sliced fresh or frozen makrut lime leaves (stems removed if thick)

1 g / ½ teaspoon kosher salt

Freshly ground black pepper

4 (12 by 9-inch / 30 by 23-cm) pieces fresh or thawed frozen banana leaf

HANG MUU YAANG

หางหมูย่าง   Grilled pig's tails

A few years back and just minutes after I showed up in Chiang Mai, my friend and culinary guru Sunny called with one of his hot tips: a restaurant in the middle of nowhere was serving old-school food. That was enough for me. Soon, he and I were in my truck rumbling past rice fields and banana trees toward the Northern Thai village of Mae On. We arrived hungry, but by the time we actually found Heuan Him Tang, we were starving. Part of our problem was that we were looking for a restaurant rather than a shack in someone's front yard. We should've known. After all, the name of the place basically means "house on the side of the road." By now, I know the way. I go back every time I make landfall.

The matriarch of the place is well-known throughout the village and beyond for her *luu* (chilled, spiced raw blood soup) and *muu yaang ruam* (grilled pig parts—snout, ears, chin, cheek, you name it). The only thing that's vegetarian here is the rice whiskey. Like so many of my favorite cooks, the secret to her success is one part good taste and ten parts hard work, with her and her family laboring over the same handful of dishes every damn day. That's the only reason I can think of to explain why she's able to make pig's tails (my favorite of all of her equally great food) that are well worth the forty-five-minute drive from Chiang Mai and maybe even the flight from Portland.

◊ ◊ ◊

A meat tenderizer

A grill, preferably charcoal (highly recommended), grate oiled

---

6 cups / 1.4 L warm tap water

50 g / ⅓ cup kosher salt

50 g / ¼ cup granulated sugar

25 g / 2 tablespoons MSG (optional but highly recommended)

3 g / 1 teaspoon black peppercorns

35 g / ¼ cup thinly sliced peeled fresh or thawed frozen galangal

24 g / 8 unpeeled garlic cloves

30 g / 30 cilantro roots

2 large stalks lemongrass, bottom 1 inch / 2.5 cm, top 9 inches / 23 cm, and outer layer removed

2 pounds / 900 g skin-on whole pig's tails

Naam Phrik Khaa (Galangal chile dip), page 67, and/or Jaew (Isaan dipping sauce), page 245, for serving

Grilled slow and long, the tails become a mosaic of tender flesh, gelatinous cartilage, creamy fat, and miscellaneous crunchy bits. By the time they leave the grate, the skin is as crispy as the crackling on Chinese suckling pig, golden brown, and puffed as if it had been fried. Hacked into pieces, they are perfect for people who love gnawing at bones. Like so much drinking food in Thailand, this dish forces you to battle a bit for the good stuff. ◊ *serves 8 to 12*

Marinate the pig's tails

Combine the water, salt, sugar, MSG, and peppercorns in a tall, narrow container and stir well to dissolve the salt, sugar, and MSG. Lightly smash the galangal with a pestle, a pan, or the flat surface of a knife blade to release the oils. Do the same to the garlic, cilantro roots, and lemongrass. Chop the lemongrass into 1-inch / 2.5-cm pieces. Add the galangal, garlic, cilantro roots, and lemongrass to the container and stir.

Prick the tails all over with the meat tenderizer (this helps the marinade penetrate the meat). Transfer the tails to the container, making sure they are submerged. Cover and refrigerate for at least 4 hours or up to 1 day.

Grill the pig's tails

Prepare the grill to cook with medium-low heat (see page 129). Remove the tails from the marinade and discard the marinade. Put the tails on the grill grate and grill, turning them occasionally and adding more charcoal as necessary to maintain the heat, until the skin is light golden brown and the tails are very tender but not falling apart, about 1¼ hours. Then continue grilling until the skin gets puffy, crispy, and lightly charred, about 15 minutes more.

Transfer the tails to a cutting board, cut crosswise into about 1-inch / 2.5-cm pieces, transfer to a plate, and serve right away with the dips.

SAI KRAWK ISAAN

Isaan fermented pork-and-rice sausages

ไส้กรอกอีสาน

Originally from Isaan, these sour pork-and-rice sausages have become a common sight on street-side grills throughout Thailand. When I say streets, I mean it. Although virtually everything unfamiliar to Americans often gets lumped into the street-food category, this particular specialty is typically hawked not by sit-down operations but by vendors parked on the sidewalk. The sausage takes two forms: as a single link impaled on a skewer or as small spheres strung together, with the latter festooning some vendor stalls as advertisement. Shapes be damned, the taste is what matters. *Sai krawk isaan* is porky and garlicky, with the sour tang from fermentation—the time-honored technique of giving certain bacteria a little running room.

Back in the day, I'd trade a few baht for a meaty link of the vendor's making. Nowadays, you can expect to find purchased sausages that are mostly rice or, in a common modern riff, glass noodles. You can expect to find hot dogs sold by these vendors as well, because they're so freaking popular. Not unsurprisingly, I prefer the old-school way, packing casings with mostly pork and just enough rice to encourage fermentation.

◊ *makes about 16 (4-inch / 10-cm) links*

◊ ◊ ◊

Make the sausages

Rinse the rice in a bowl of room-temperature tap water to cool it down, breaking up clumps, then drain very well.

Combine the pork shoulder, pork belly, curing powder, rice, garlic, pepper, sugar, and chile powder in a large bowl and use your hands to mix until well combined.

Rinse the casings well under running cold water, then rinse the insides by putting one end of each casing around the mouth of the faucet and letting the water run through it for a few minutes. This will also show you whether the casing is broken. Use about 8 feet / 1.5 m of unbroken casings for your sausage (though a continuous length of 8 feet / 1.5 m is not necessary). Discard any broken casing—that's why you bought so much.

If you have a sausage maker, good for you. If not, you can stuff the casings with the help of a sausage-stuffer funnel. First, insert the narrow end of the funnel into the open end of the casing. Next, tie a tight knot at the other end of the casing, and then gather as much of the casing as you can onto the funnel. Push the meat, a few tablespoons at a time, through the funnel and into the casing. When you have a good 6 inches / 15 cm or so of meat in the casing, stop for a moment, hold the open end of the casing with one hand, and use the other hand to gently but firmly force the meat toward the knotted end. Before you twist the sausage into links, you want to make sure you have a good 8 inches / 20 cm or so of empty casing left at the open end.

Using a toothpick or a thin wooden skewer, prick the casing near any air bubbles you spot. Then slowly run one hand along the sausage from the open end to the knotted end to ensure the meat is as evenly distributed as possible and to eliminate any remaining air pockets. Prick the casing every inch / 2.5 cm so the sausage won't burst when you cook it.

Starting at the tied end of the casing, twist the sausage into 4-inch / 10-cm links. Each time you twist, tie a piece of the kitchen twine around the twist to secure it. Wipe the outsides of the sausages with a damp towel and then dry them.

◊ ◊ ◊

SPECIAL EQUIPMENT

A sausage maker or sausage-stuffer funnel

Kitchen twine, cut into 15 (3-inch / 7.5-cm) lengths

A grill, preferably charcoal (highly recommended), grate oiled, if grilling

A deep-fry thermometer, if frying

———

650 g / 3½ cups freshly cooked Khao Niaw (Sticky rice), page 248

1 pound, 2 ounces / 500 g pork shoulder, ground through a ⅜-inch / 1-cm die by you or your butcher

1 pound, 2 ounces / 500 g pork belly, ground through a ⅜-inch / 1-cm die by you or your butcher

20 g / 1½ tablespoons Tusino-style curing powder (such as Lee or Por Kwan brand)

85 g / ½ cup peeled garlic cloves, minced

8 g / 3½ teaspoons ground white pepper (from an Asian market)

7 g / 1½ teaspoons granulated sugar

Less than 1 g / ½ teaspoon Phrik Pon Khua (Toasted-chile powder), page 233

About 9 feet / 2.7 m natural hog or beef middle sausage casings, thawed if frozen or soaked in water for 5 minutes if salted

Neutral oil (such as soybean or palm), if deep-frying (about 12 cups / 2.8 L)

To Serve Alongside

White cabbage wedges

Unsalted roasted peanuts

Peeled fresh ginger, thinly sliced against the grain

Fresh Thai chiles

Ferment the sausages

Hang the links and ferment according to the directions on page 110 until the meat has achieved the sourness you prefer. This will take up to 2 days, depending on the ambient temperature and your preference. Sniff the links to assess their progress.

At this point, you can wrap the links in plastic wrap and store them in the refrigerator for up to 5 days or put them in freezer bags and freeze them for up to 3 months. Before cooking them, cut between each link to separate them.

Cook and serve the sausages

To grill: Prepare the grill to cook with medium heat (see page 129). Grill the links, turning occasionally, until lightly browned and cooked through, 5 to 8 minutes.

To fry: Select a heavy pot at least 12 inches / 30 cm wide and pour in the oil to a depth of 2 to 3 inches / 5 to 7.5 cm. Set the pot over high heat and heat the oil to 350°F / 180°C. Use the thermometer to test the temperature, measuring the oil at the center of the vessel and carefully stirring the oil occasionally to ensure a consistent temperature. Line a large sheet pan with paper towels or newspaper and set it near the stove.

Working in batches if needed to avoid crowding the oil, add the sausages to the hot oil and fry until lightly browned and cooked through, 2 to 3 minutes. Using tongs, transfer them to the prepared pan to drain. Repeat with the remaining sausages.

Let the sausages cool slightly, then slice into bite-size pieces. Serve with the cabbage, peanuts, ginger, and chiles for eating between bites of sausage.

TAP KAI / TAP PET PING

Grilled chicken / duck liver skewers   ตับไก่ / ตับเป็ดปิ้ง

When I stagger onto the street after one-too-many whiskeys, I follow the smell of charcoal smoke to the vendors selling chicken parts on wooden skewers. Next to a rudimentary brazier, there's probably a banana leaf–lined table with all manner of charred meat and offal along with, perhaps, whole fish and small sausage links. Spend some time watching the operation and you might be surprised to see a customer grab a couple of skewers and place them on the grill himself to warm them up. Now that's not something you'd see at a New York City kebab cart.

These grilled-meat depositories are typically run by people from Isaan, who have left their homes in the traditionally poor Northeast to find work, often manual labor. During the day, you'll find these setups near construction sites, outside factories, and next to other places where Isaan workers toil. The food is cheap, a few baht a skewer, and damn good. Some vendors set out a stack of herbs for the taking, as well as an array of condiments, sauces, and *naam phrik*, fiery and pungent all of them. Chicken livers (or duck livers, if you can find them) are one of my go-to skewers. Treat them right—a garlic-and-cilantro-root marinade and fiery, aromatic *jaew* for dipping—and they will treat you right.

◊ *makes about 6 skewers*

◊ ◊ ◊

SPECIAL EQUIPMENT

A Thai granite mortar and pestle

6 wooden skewers, each about 8 inches / 20 cm long, soaked in tepid water for 30 minutes

A grill, preferably charcoal (highly recommended), grate oiled

Rinse the livers under cold running water and drain well. Trim off the string-like parts and blood clots, then cut the livers into about 1-inch / 2.5-cm pieces.

Combine the garlic, cilantro roots, and peppercorns in the mortar and pound to a fine paste, about 1 minute. Scrape the paste into a bowl. Add the thin soy sauce, sweet soy sauce, and sugar and stir well. Add the livers and toss to coat evenly. Cover and marinate in the fridge for at least 1 hour or up to 2 hours.

While the livers marinate, prepare the grill to cook with medium-high heat (see page 129).

Thread 5 or 6 liver pieces onto each skewer, making sure the tip of the skewer isn't exposed (otherwise it will burn) and leaving a few inches of empty space at the bottom of the skewer. Grill the skewers without messing with them, until the liver releases easily from the grate, 2 to 3 minutes. Turn the skewers and continue to grill, flipping them only as needed to avoid becoming very dark, until the liver is just slightly pink in the center, 2 to 3 minutes more. Cooks in Thailand would keep grilling until they are fully cooked, but I like them this way.

Transfer to a plate and serve right away with the dipping sauce.

1 pound / 455 g chicken or duck livers

15 g / 5 peeled garlic cloves, halved lengthwise

3 g / 3 cilantro roots

4 g / 1½ teaspoons black peppercorns

3 tablespoons Thai thin soy sauce

1½ teaspoons Thai sweet soy sauce

3 g / ¾ teaspoon granulated sugar

¼ cup / 60 ml Jaew (Isaan dipping sauce), page 245

KUNG PHAO

Grilled prawns   กุ้งเผา

White sand, clear blue water, palm trees—it's the Thailand of postcards and of beach vacations in places like Koh Samui, Krabi, and Phuket. For many travelers, it's where they have their first Thai food revelation, when they realize that the cuisine transcends the pleasures of phat thai and green curry. Before I fell for the food of the landlocked North, I found bliss in the coastal resorts down south, where life seemed as simple as the bungalows were cheap and the drinks were cold. The food at the huts and other beachfront operations tends to be straightforward seafood preparations like this one: shrimp, shells and heads on, cooked over charcoal and so full of sea flavor they don't even need a sprinkle of salt. A few beers and a little bowl of *naam jim* made from lots of grilled chiles, garlic, lime juice, and fish sauce complete the picture. No wonder so many people come for a week and stay for a month. ◊ *serves 4 to 6*

Prepare the grill to cook with medium-high heat (see page 129). Grill the prawns, turning them once, until their shells turn bright pink and are slightly charred and they are just cooked through, 6 to 8 minutes.

Transfer to a plate and serve right away with the dipping sauce.

SPECIAL EQUIPMENT
A grill, preferably charcoal (highly recommended), grate oiled

12 to 16 shell-on, head-on giant prawns (about 2 pounds / 900 g)

½ cup / 120 ml Naam Jim Seafood (Spicy, tart dipping sauce for seafood), page 243

JIN SOM
MOK KHAI

จิ้นส้มหมกไข่   Sour pork and egg grilled in banana leaves

Up North, there are villages where making *jin som* (sour meat) is the local cottage industry, just as others specialize in crafting *laap* knives or producing *khanom jiin* (fermented rice noodles). In San Sai, I spent hours watching a group of about eight women boil and slice pork skin, then mix it with ground pork, sticky rice, garlic, salt, and MSG. A few of the women sit on splayed cardboard boxes, using their hands to scoop the mixture onto several layers of banana leaves cut from nearby trees. They fold the leaves around the mixture rather elaborately to ensure the meat has no exposure to air and then secure the bundles with rubber bands.

The first time I visited, I learned, to my surprise, that these women don't ferment the meat. Instead, they sell their product to vendors at markets and to restaurant owners who undertake the wildly complex process of fermentation themselves. In Thailand, that process goes as follows: Leave the bundles out for a few days until they're sour but not too sour. The higher the temperature, the faster the progression will be. The salt restrains the bacteria, so the meat ferments but doesn't cross into unpleasant territory. At one of my preferred *jin som* peddlers, Paa Daeng Jin Tup, near Chiang Mai, the sourness varies depending on whether or not everything was sold out the night before. If any is left over, it will ferment further as it sits out until the next evening. I like *jin som* both fairly fresh (when it's mild and has a softer texture) and not (when the sourness intensifies and the texture tightens). Either way, when it's grilled inside

banana leaves along with a chicken or duck egg, it's as delicious as anything I've ever eaten.

Unless *jin som* is your cottage industry, the process is a pain in the ass. So this recipe produces a big batch. Once fermented, it keeps in the fridge for up to 1 week and in the freezer for up to 3 months. ◊ ***makes 14 to 16***

◊ ◊ ◊

Khawng Yaang: Grilled Foods

14 to 16 rubber bands

A grill, preferably charcoal (highly recommended), grate oiled

14 to 16 wooden toothpicks, soaked in tepid water for 30 minutes

185 g / 1 cup freshly cooked Khao Niaw (Sticky rice), page 248

2¼ pounds / 1 kg skin-on pork fatback, cut lengthwise into pieces 2 inches / 5 cm wide

1 pound, 2 ounces / 500 g boneless, skinless pork leg, coarsely ground by your butcher

125 g / ¾ cup peeled garlic cloves, minced

35 g / 2 tablespoons iodized salt

25 g / 2 tablespoons MSG (optional but highly recommended)

56 (12 by 9-inch / 30 by 23-cm) pieces fresh or thawed frozen banana leaf (from about 3 packages)

14 chicken or duck eggs at room temperature

To Serve Alongside

Fresh Thai chiles

Raw mild garlic cloves

Assemble the packets

Rinse the rice in a bowl of room-temperature tap water to cool it down, breaking up clumps, then drain very well.

Put the pork fatback in a pot, add water to cover by about 1 inch / 2.5 cm, and generously salt the water as if you were cooking pasta. Set the pot over high heat and bring the water to a strong simmer. Decrease the heat to maintain a gentle but steady simmer and cook, skimming off any surface scum, until the skin is translucent and the fat is soft enough to easily slice but is not falling apart, about 30 minutes.

Drain well, transfer to a large bowl, and add enough water to submerge the pork fat. When the pieces are just cool enough to handle but still warm, remove them from the water and trim and discard any flesh if necessary. Slice the pieces crosswise into strips about 2 inches (5 cm) long and 1/16 inch (2 mm) wide.

Combine the fatback slices, ground pork, rice, garlic, salt, and MSG in a large bowl and use your hands to mix until all of the ingredients are well distributed.

On a work surface, stack 4 banana leaf pieces, with the first piece shiny side down and the fourth piece shiny side up. Put about 115 g / ½ cup of the meat mixture in the center of the stack and fold according to the photos, opposite. Secure the packet with a rubber band. Repeat to make more packets until all of the meat mixture is used. You should have 14 packets.

Ferment the pork

Ferment the packets according to the directions on page 110, flipping the packets twice a day, until the meat has achieved the sourness you prefer, 24 to 48 hours, depending on the ambient temperature and your preference. Open one of the parcels occasionally to check on the progress, sniffing the meat to assess the sourness.

Grill the packets

Prepare the grill to cook with medium-low heat (see page 129).

Remove the rubber band from a packet and unwrap enough to reveal the pork. Crack an egg into the packet, refold loosely, and secure with a toothpick (do not puncture the part of the packet that contains the pork). Repeat with the remaining packets and eggs.

Put the packets, seam side up, on the grill grate and grill, without flipping them, until the pork is hot and the egg white has set but the yolk is still molten (feel free to peek inside the packets), 15 to 17 minutes.

Serve right away with the chiles and garlic for eating between bites, letting people open the packets themselves.

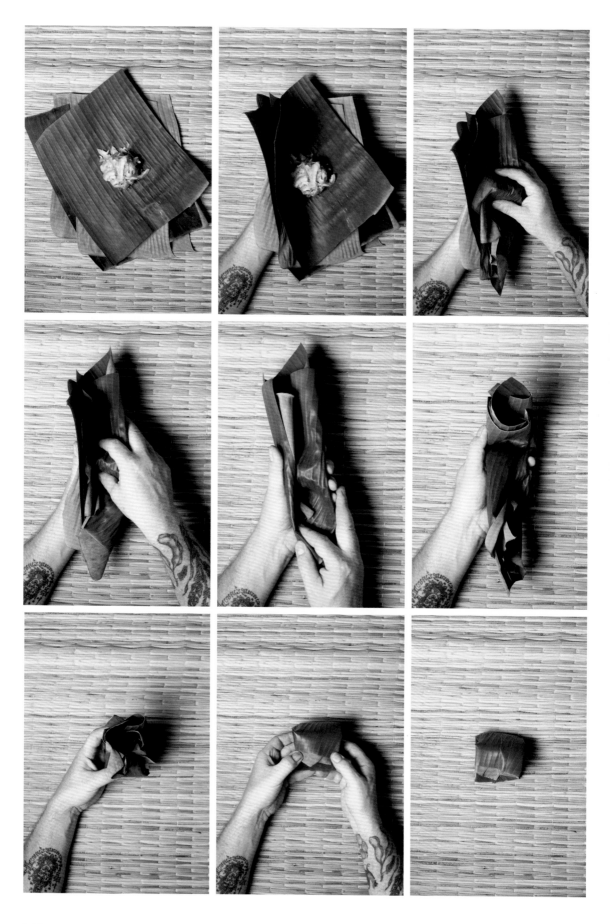

WHISKEY SODA

In Thailand, especially in its more cosmopolitan precincts, there's a thriving cocktail culture, but odds are, when you're having a mixed drink in the country, it's whiskey soda. That's what Thais call the mixture of, you guessed it, whiskey and soda. The tipple is such an iconic part of revelry in Thailand that when I opened a bar in Portland, Oregon, that trafficked in the world of *aahaan kap klaem*, I called it Whiskey Soda Lounge.

The way the drink is typically served would probably qualify as posh at a bar in the States—a low-end version of bottle service. In Thailand, it's just the way things are done. Say you're meeting your friends for a drink at a proper bar—in contrast to the makeshift stalls selling spirits like *ya dawng* and *lao khao*—and you all order whiskey soda. Your waiter will probably arrive minutes later with a segmented plastic crate, the slots filled with a bottle of brown liquor, soda water, and glasses for everyone at your table. The waiter will set up a folding table to hold the fixings and a bucket of ice, then proceed to make drinks, stirring each one with the tongs from the ice bucket. He'll return to do the same whenever the levels look low. A comely young woman will perform these tasks if the customer is male and happens to choose a bar haunted by the hired guns paid by liquor companies to push one brand or another.

Despite the cocktail's name, the spirit isn't always technically whiskey. A liter of 100 Pipers, for instance, really is whiskey—albeit blended and not exactly high-test stuff—but the ubiquitous Sang Som or Mekhong are only colloquially so. They're made mostly from sugarcane and are therefore essentially rums. No matter. They're brown, and when they're sufficiently watered down, they taste a bit like whiskey anyway. For those of us who occasionally blow eighty bucks on a bottle of single malt, the primary purpose of booze bears remembering.

You would be well advised to show up in Thailand with a couple of bottles in their suitcases. Import taxes make good whiskey, bourbon, and the like extremely expensive in Thailand, and showing up at a bar with something as commonplace in the States as Maker's Mark will make you the most popular guy at the table. That, by the way, is another cool reality of drinking in Thailand: many bars are BYOB.

At a fancy nightclub in Bangkok, you'd have to splurge on Johnnie Walker. But at the average up-country drinking joint, where 100 Pipers counts as top-shelf stuff, you're welcome to bring your own bottle and just pay for the mixers, just as many restaurants there let you bring mangoes for dessert and will even peel them for you. When you leave, you take the bottle with you, at least if you haven't finished it.

YAM
SALADS
ยำ

SUP NAW MAI

ชุปหน่อไม้   Isaan bamboo shoot salad

Most of us have enjoyed slivers of bamboo shoots floating in curries, but to eat a dish centered around the vegetable reminds you that it can taste pretty funky. In this Isaan preparation, it's the main event, the flavor matched with a pungent dressing of lime, fish sauce, toasted-rice powder, and dried chile. In addition, there's the vegetal, slightly astringent juice of *yanang* leaf, an ingredient often omitted by the kinds of modern Isaan restaurants you see in Bangkok or Chiang Mai, but which is, to my mind, an essential component of the dish.

The leaf—more common in the cooking of Laos and a reminder that many people of the Northeast of Thailand are ethnically Lao—is so closely associated with bamboo shoots that you'll often spot the jarred shoots packed with *yanang* juice. This is a decent option, as are plain "bamboo shoot tips" in brine or vacuum-packed tips, as long as you rinse them before using. You don't, however, want "sour" or "pickled" bamboo shoots for this recipe. And if given the choice, pick shoots that are closer to white, because yellow or darker ones tend to be tougher and have a stronger flavor.

If fresh bamboo shoots are hard to locate in the United States, fresh *yanang* leaves are nearly impossible to get your mitts on. You'll find the juice in cans, but I recommend seeking out the frozen leaves and blending them with water to make your own. ◊ *serves 4 to 6*

◊ ◊ ◊

A grill, preferably charcoal (highly recommended), grate oiled

2 or 3 wooden skewers, soaked in tepid water for 30 minutes

2 or 3 wooden toothpicks, soaked in tepid water for 30 minutes, if using banana leaf

A Thai granite mortar and pestle

Paste

40 g unpeeled garlic cloves

35 g unpeeled Asian shallots

1 (12 by 9-inch / 30 by 23-cm) piece fresh or thawed frozen banana leaf, halved crosswise (optional)

21 g pickled gouramy fish fillets

25 g stemmed fresh serrano chiles

Make the paste

Prepare the grill to cook with medium-high heat (see page 129). Thread the garlic and shallots onto separate skewers. If you're using the banana leaf, stack the halves. Alternatively, create a double layer of aluminum foil of about the same size. Put the gouramy fillets on the center of the banana leaf or foil, fold the sides in to make a packet, and secure closed with the toothpicks.

Put the chiles on the grill grate and grill, turning them frequently and occasionally pressing them so they cook evenly, until completely blistered and almost completely blackened all over and the flesh is fully soft but not mushy, 15 to 25 minutes. Transfer to a plate.

Raise the height of the grill grate and flatten the bed of coals, or let the coals cool slightly to cook with medium heat. Put the gouramy packet, garlic, and shallots on the grill grate and grill, transferring them to a plate as they are ready: Cook the gouramy packet, turning it occasionally, just until you can smell the floral funk of the gouramy, about 15 minutes. Cook the garlic and shallots, turning them occasionally, until they are charred in spots and fully soft but still hold their shape, 15 to 25 minutes. Let the chiles, shallots, and garlic cool to room temperature. Use your fingers or a small knife to stem and peel the chiles, shallots, and garlic.

While the garlic, shallots, and chiles are cooling, open the gouramy packet, discard any large bones and fins (don't try to remove the small bones), and transfer the remainder to the mortar. Firmly pound until a paste forms and the bones have fully broken down, about 45 seconds. Add the garlic to the mortar and pound to a thick, fairly fine sludge, about 1 minute. Do the same with the shallots, about 2 minutes, and then with the chiles, about 2 minutes.

Reserve 21 g / 1 heaping tablespoon of the paste for this recipe. Store the remaining paste in an airtight container in the fridge for up to 1 week or in the freezer for up to 6 months.

Make the salad

Combine the *yanang* leaves in a blender with 1 cup of water and blend until smooth. Strain through a fine-mesh strainer into a measuring cup, pressing the solids to release as much liquid as possible. Reserve ¼ cup plus 2 tablespoons of the liquid.

Combine the *yanang* liquid, fish sauce, lime juice, chile powder, and reserved paste in a saucepan, stir, and bring to a boil over high heat. Add the bamboo shoots, turn down the heat to low, and cook gently just until the bamboo shoots are warmed through, about 2 minutes. Let the mixture cool until just warm.

Transfer the salad (including all of the dressing) to a plate in a low heap. Sprinkle on the cilantro, sawtooth herb, green onions, and mint and then top with the sesame seeds and rice powder. Serve right away.

Salad

30 g / ½ cup crumbled frozen yanang leaves

1 tablespoon Thai fish sauce

1 tablespoon fresh lime juice, preferably from Key limes or from regular (Persian) limes spiked with a small squeeze of Meyer lemon juice

1 g / 1 teaspoon Phrik Pon Khua (Toasted-chile powder), page 233

55 g / 1 cup drained shredded Thai bamboo shoots, rinsed

2 g / 1 tablespoon coarsely chopped cilantro (thin stems and leaves)

2 g / 1 tablespoon thinly sliced sawtooth herb

5 g / 1 tablespoon sliced (¼ inch / 6 mm) green onions

3 g / ¼ cup small mint leaves

2 g / ½ teaspoon toasted sesame seeds

9 g / 1 tablespoon Khao Khua (Toasted–sticky rice powder), page 232

Shown here is *yam plaa meuk*, poached squid salad.

YAM PLAA MEUK

ยำปลาหมึก   Squid salad

This one is dead simple: squid tossed with herbs in a fiercely hot mixture of chiles, garlic, lime juice, and fish sauce—its razor-sharp edge just barely blunted by a touch of sugar. It takes no special know-how to reproduce this dish, the kind that would have you dabbing your brow at one of the seedy spots around Bangkok's Sukhumvit Road. With the dressing made and the ingredients prepped, your only task is not overcooking the squid, a job made easy by gentle, brief poaching (Thais call this cooking technique *luak*). Turning the tubular bodies of the cephalopod inside out also helps to make each bite particularly tender. ◊ *serves 4*

Bring a pot of water to a boil over high heat, then lower the heat to maintain a very gentle simmer. You're after tiny bubbles that don't break the surface (160°F to 180°F /71°C to 82°C).

Meanwhile, separate the squid tentacles from the bodies. Turn each squid body inside out, then cut into rings ½ inch / 12 mm wide. Put the squid in the long-handled noodle basket or deep strainer.

Pound the garlic and chiles in the mortar to a very coarse paste, about 15 seconds. Transfer 18 g / 1½ tablespoons of the mixture (or more to taste) to a saucepan and add the lime juice, fish sauce, and sugar. Set it over medium heat and heat the mixture just until warm to the touch, 15 seconds or so. Turn off the heat.

Generously season the simmering water with kosher salt as if you were cooking pasta. Dip the noodle basket in the water, submerging the squid fully, and cook, gently shaking the basket constantly to keep the squid moving around, just until cooked through, about 10 seconds. Shake the basket to drain well.

Add the squid, tomatoes, white onion, celery, green onions, and cilantro to the saucepan holding the paste and toss well. Transfer the salad (including all of the dressing) to a plate in a low heap. Serve right away.

SPECIAL EQUPIMENT

A long-handled noodle basket or a deep strainer

A Thai granite mortar and pestle

---

4 ounces / 115 g cleaned small squid

14 g / 4 peeled garlic cloves, halved lengthwise

6 g / 4 stemmed fresh Thai chiles, preferably green

3 tablespoons fresh lime juice, preferably from Key limes or from regular (Persian) limes spiked with a small squeeze of Meyer lemon juice

2 tablespoons Thai fish sauce

4 g / 1 teaspoon granulated sugar

Kosher salt

2 ounces / 55 g cherry tomatoes (about 4 tomatoes), halved, or quartered if very large

30 g / ¼ cup thinly sliced (with the grain) peeled white onion

6 g / ¼ cup coarsely chopped Chinese celery (thin stems and leaves)

10 g / 2 tablespoons sliced (¼ inch / 6 mm) green onions

2 g / 1 tablespoon coarsely chopped cilantro (thin stems and leaves)

YAM PLAA SALIT

ยำปลาสลิด   Fried gouramy fish salad

Note on Plaa Salit: Look for these salted fish in the cooler or freezer section of Asian markets. Occasionally labeled "snakeskin fish" or "gouramy fish," they are typically sold in bags of four to eight fish, gutted and headless but otherwise whole, including bones, tails, and fins. Although they are salted, handling them will feel like handling raw fresh fish, as they are neither especially firm nor dry.

If you're lucky, on a night when you get truly hammered, some wise soul will lead you off of Thanon Charoen Krung, one of Bangkok Chinatown's raucous main drags, to Khao Tom Jay Suay. Even though the place has been around for about fifty years, locals refer to it as Khao Tom Roy Pee ("Hundred-Year-Old Khao Tom"). The nickname is probably a comment on the quality of food, which is so good that you can imagine it coming from cooks with a century's worth of practice. It might as well be a comment on the elderly "shop house" of which the restaurant occupies the ground floor.

You find a stool at a curbside table. The side street is fragrant in the way you'd think a street in a city of more than eight million people where the temperature often tops 100°F / 38° C would be. The mode of eating here could be characterized as *khao tom kui*, several dishes served alongside bowls of liquidy rice porridge—a different style of *khao tom* than the flavorful one-bowl meal featured on page 214. You order some *jap chai* (soupy stewed mustard greens with a few hunks of pork) and a variety of prepared meats, including slices of smoked duck, if you know what you're doing. You order a stir-fry made to order from the variety of vegetables (like *phak krachet*, water mimosa) laid out in a couple dozen bowls arranged on the table in front of the restaurant. This is typical *khao tom* restaurant fare. It's not necessarily what most people expect to eat in Thailand. In fact, it's essentially Chinese food, almost completely free from the heat of chiles but packed with flavor nonetheless.

◊ ◊ ◊

A deep-fry thermometer

A large spider skimmer
(recommended)

A Thai granite mortar and
pestle

———

Neutral oil (such as soybean
or palm), for deep-frying
(about 12 cups /2.8 L)

1 (5-ounce / 140 g) salted
fresh or thawed frozen plaa
salit (see Note, page 174)

50 g / ¼ cup plus
3 tablespoons Asian white
rice flour (not glutinous
rice flour)

14 g / 4 peeled garlic cloves,
halved lengthwise

6 g / 4 stemmed fresh Thai
chiles, preferably green

2 tablespoons fresh lime
juice, preferably from
Key limes or from regular
(Persian) limes spiked with
a small squeeze of Meyer
lemon juice

1 tablespoon Thai fish
sauce

2 g / ½ teaspoon
granulated sugar

45 g / ⅓ cup peeled thinly
sliced (with the grain)
white onion

6 g / ¼ cup coarsely
chopped Chinese celery
(thin stems and leaves)

10 g / 2 tablespoons sliced
(¼ inch / 6 mm) green
onions

2 g / 1 tablespoon coarsely
chopped cilantro (thin
stems and leaves)

Yet you'll also see dishes at Khao Tom Jay Suay that possess the spicy, sour, salty flavors that so many *farang* have come to recognize as Thai. Case in point: This *yam* in the mold of other Central Thai "salads" with its lime-, garlic-, and chile-spiked dressing and fresh blast of herbs. The highlight of this particular version is *plaa salit*, a small freshwater fish that's been cured with salt, dredged in rice flour, then deep-fried, bones and all, until it has not the crackling exterior of fish and chips, but the through-and-through crunch of a chip. It's a true pleasure, whether it's accompanied by rice porridge to prevent a hangover or enjoyed on its own with enough booze to bring one on.

◊ *serves 4*

Select a heavy pot at least 12 inches / 30 cm wide and pour in the oil to a depth of 2 inches / 5 cm. Set the pot over high heat and heat the oil to 350°F / 180°C. Use the thermometer to test the temperature, measuring the oil at the center of the vessel and carefully stirring the oil occasionally to ensure a consistent temperature. Line a sheet pan with paper towels or newspaper and put it near the stove.

While the oil is heating, turn the fish belly up. Using a large, sharp knife, cut the fish in half lengthwise through the spine (your goal is to split the bone in two, though perfection isn't necessary), then cut the halves across the spine into strips ¾ inch / 2 cm wide. Do not remove the bones or fins.

Dump the rice flour into a wide bowl. Add the fish pieces and toss to coat with a thin layer of flour, shaking off any excess. Carefully add the fish to the hot oil and fry until light brown and completely crunchy (not just the exterior but all the way through), 12 to 15 minutes. Using the spider or a slotted spoon, transfer the fish to the prepared pan.

Pound the garlic and chiles in the mortar to a very coarse paste, about 15 seconds. Transfer 12 g / 1 tablespoon of the mixture (or more to taste) to a saucepan and add the lime juice, fish sauce, and sugar. Set it over medium heat and heat the mixture just until warm to the touch, 15 seconds or so. Turn off the heat, add the fried fish, white onion, celery, green onions, and cilantro, and toss well.

Transfer the salad (including all of the dressing) to a plate in a low heap. Serve right away.

YAM WUN SEN

Glass noodle salad   ยำวุ้นเส้น

You are likely to see *yam wun sen*, a salad of glass noodles, at housewarming parties and other celebratory events. Noodles are believed to bring luck, their length representing long life. Befitting the special occasion, good cooks make *chao wang* (fancy) versions, kitting out the dish with prawns, ground pork, and both fried shallots and garlic. But roll up to a bar and you'll find a very different version of *yam wun sen*. The salad's booze-friendly alter ego contains only the basics—glass noodles, herbs, sliced shallots, and dried shrimp—and some *muu yaw* (essentially Thai bologna) to keep things classy. The noodles won't be tossed in a carefully calibrated dressing but in a blazing-hot, bracingly sour, garlicky mixture that will keep you reaching for beer. ◊ *serves 4 to 6*

Note on Glass Noodles and Vietnamese Pork Roll: Also called mung bean, bean thread, or cellophane noodles, glass noodles (*wun sen*) are sold dried in bags at Asian markets and many supermarkets. When rehydrated, they have a transparent appearance and slightly gelatinous texture. Vietnamese pork roll (*muu yaw* in Thai) is a slightly spongy, cold-cut-like pork product sold at Vietnamese and other Southeast Asian markets, typically in the refrigerated section. Most likely, it will be labeled chả lụa, giò lụa, or another approximate spelling of the Vietnamese.

◊ ◊ ◊

1 (2-ounce) piece
Vietnamese pork roll
(See Note, page 177)
quartered

Dressing

14 g / 4 peeled garlic cloves,
halved lengthwise

6 g / 4 stemmed fresh Thai
chiles, preferably red

1 tablespoon plus
1 teaspoon fresh lime
juice, preferably from
Key limes or from regular
(Persian) limes spiked
with a small squeeze of
Meyer lemon juice

1 tablespoon plus
1 teaspoon Thai fish sauce

2 teaspoons liquid from
Thai jarred pickled garlic

2 teaspoons water

3 g / ¾ teaspoon
granulated sugar

Salad

1¼ ounces / 35 g dried
glass noodles (see Note,
page 177), soaked in
lukewarm water until very
pliable, about 8 minutes,
drained well, and snipped
into irregular 4- to 6-inch /
10- to 15-cm lengths

1 (2-ounce / 55-g) piece
Vietnamese pork roll (see
Note, page 177), quartered
lengthwise and cut into
slices ⅛ inch / 3 mm thick

1 tablespoon Naam Man
Krathiam (Fried garlic oil),
page 234, or Naam Man
Hom Jiaw (Fried shallot oil),
page 235

14 g / ¼ cup peeled carrot
cut into matchsticks about
3 by ⅛ inch / 7.5 cm by
3 mm

16 g / 2 tablespoons thinly
sliced (with the grain)
peeled Asian shallots

4 g / 2 tablespoons
coarsely chopped cilantro
(thin stems and leaves),
plus pinch for finishing

3 g / 2 tablespoons
coarsely chopped Chinese
celery (thin stems and
leaves)

7 g / 1 tablespoon Kung
Haeng Khua (Dry-fried
dried shrimp), page 239

8 g / 1 tablespoon very
thinly sliced (crosswise)
unpeeled jarred pickled
garlic head

Pinch of ground white
pepper (from an Asian
market)

5 g / 1 tablespoon
Krathiam Jiaw (Fried garlic),
page 234

Make the dressing

Combine the garlic and chiles in the mortar and pound to a very coarse
paste, about 15 seconds. Transfer 8 g / 2 teaspoons of the mixture (or
more to taste) to a saucepan and add the lime juice, fish sauce, pickled
garlic liquid, water, and sugar. Set aside for the moment.

Make the salad

Bring a pot of water to a boil over high heat, then lower the heat to
maintain a gentle simmer. Put the noodles and pork roll in the noodle
basket and put the basket in the water. Cook, gently shaking the basket
frequently to move the ingredients around, just until the noodles are
tender, about 30 seconds. Firmly shake the basket to drain well.

Set the saucepan containing the chile mixture over medium heat and
heat the mixture just until warm to the touch, 15 seconds or so. Turn off
the heat. Add the noodles, pork roll, and garlic oil to the chile mixture
and toss well. Add the carrot, shallots, cilantro, celery, shrimp, pickled
garlic, and white pepper and toss well once more.

Transfer the salad (including all of the dressing) to a plate in a low heap
and sprinkle with the fried garlic and a pinch of cilantro. Stir again
before eating.

SPECIAL EQUIPMENT

A Thai granite mortar
and pestle

A long-handled noodle
basket

YAM MAMA

ยำมาม่า   Instant-noodle salad

A modern classic, this Thai *yam* is made from noodles repurposed from a package of instant ramen. The product is beloved in Thailand, so much so that noodle-soup spots offer the desiccated bricks alongside options freshly made from rice or wheat. That someone, somewhere, thought to cook the ubiquitous noodles and dress them with lime, fish sauce, and chiles was inevitable. The dish exemplifies the governing principle of drinking-food creation: to turn what's lying around into something that goes well with booze. By that measure, *yam mama* is actually quite sophisticated. Plenty of inebriates skip all the pomp—the dressing, the herbs and vegetables, and the spongy Vietnamese pork roll and smattering of shrimp— and instead just bust open a package and crunch on the noodles. (I've seen it. Hell, I've done it.) By the way, there's no need to seek out the dish's namesake MAMA brand, whose omnipresence in Thailand has made it the Kleenex of instant noodles. ◊ ***serves 4***

Bring a small pot filled with water to a boil over high heat.

Meanwhile, pound the garlic and chiles in the mortar to a very coarse paste, about 15 seconds. Transfer 12 g / 1 tablespoon of the mixture (or more to taste) to a saucepan and add the lime juice, fish sauce, and sugar.

When the water is boiling, add the noodles and cook, stirring occasionally, until fully tender (not al dente), about 2 to 3 minutes. Turn off the heat, add the shrimp and pork roll, stir to mix, and then drain well.

Set the saucepan with the garlic-chile mixture over medium heat and heat the mixture just until warm to the touch, 15 seconds or so. Turn off the heat and add the noodles, shrimp, pork roll, shallots, white onion, tomatoes, mint, green onions, celery, and cilantro and toss well.

Transfer the salad (including all of the dressing) to a plate in a low heap. Serve right away.

14 g / 4 peeled garlic cloves, halved lengthwise

6 g / 4 stemmed fresh Thai chiles, preferably green

2 tablespoons fresh lime juice, preferably from Key limes or from regular (Persian) limes spiked with a small squeeze of Meyer lemon juice

2 tablespoons Thai fish sauce

4 g / 1 teaspoon granulated sugar

1 (2¼-ounce / 60 g) package instant ramen-style noodles, flavor package discarded

4 medium-size shrimp, peeled and halved lengthwise

1 (2-ounce / 55-g) piece Vietnamese pork roll (see Note, page 177), halved lengthwise and cut into slices ⅛ inch / 3 mm thick

8 g / 1 tablespoon thinly sliced (with the grain) peeled Asian shallots

55 g / ¼ cup thinly sliced (with the grain) peeled white onion

2 ounces / 55 g cherry tomatoes (about 4 tomatoes), halved, or quartered if very large

3 g / ¼ cup small mint leaves

10 g / 2 tablespoons sliced (¼ inch / 6 mm) green onions

3 g / 2 tablespoons coarsely chopped Chinese celery (thin stems and leaves)

2 g / 1 tablespoon coarsely chopped cilantro (thin stems and leaves)

Almost anything can become *yam*, even rehydrated Chinese dried fungus, aka mouse ear mushroom, whose slightly crunchy texture and ability to hold lots of fiery dressing makes for perfect drinking food.

YAM HET HUU NUU KHAO

ยำเห็ดหูหนูขาว   Mouse ear mushroom salad

Many years ago, after all of the bars in Chiang Mai closed, everyone went to a place called Spicy—at least, it felt like everyone. Once midnight came and serving drinks without a special license was a no-go, local restaurant workers, rock and rollers, expats, backpackers, sex workers, and transvestites—anyone still up for carousing—settled up tabs around town and converged on the picnic tables beside a little shanty on the moat road, near Tha Pae Gate. I'm not sure why Spicy was exempt from the Thai blue laws that governed similar operations. Rumor was that it was either owned by police or had paid them off. Whatever the case, it was the only game in town.

Today, Spicy has a different location, and it's more smoky, sketchy nightclub than quirky, convivial gathering spot. And today, I'm no longer constitutionally inclined to stay out past midnight. But I still think fondly of its old iteration, its vibe, and its food. It's where I first had this unforgettable dish made from something slick and snappy—almost like thinly shaved, curled cartilage. A closer look revealed that this textural marvel was *het huu nuu khao* (white mouse ear mushroom), sold in dried puffs that resemble coral and labeled appetizingly as white or snow fungus in the States. It's perfect salad fodder, since the frills of the fungus trap the viciously hot dressing, so each bite is charged with the power of lime, fish sauce, raw garlic, and fresh chile. ◊ *serves 4*

Note on White Fungus: Also labeled silver fungus or snow fungus and known as *het huu nuu* (mouse ear mushroom) in Thai, white fungus is sold dried at Asian markets. If you have the option, let price be your guide to quality. To rehydrate the fungus for this dish, soak it in plenty of lukewarm water, weighing down floaters to keep them submerged, until softened but still very crunchy, at least 1 hour or up to overnight. Trim the woody base before proceeding with the recipe.

Heat the oil in a saucepan over medium-high heat until it shimmers. Add the pork and cook, stirring and breaking up the meat and adding the dashes of fish sauce about halfway through, just until cooked, 1 to 2 minutes. Let the pork cool slightly in the saucepan.

Combine the garlic and chiles in the mortar and pound to a very coarse paste, about 15 seconds. Transfer 18 g / 1½ tablespoons of the chile mixture (or more to taste) to the saucepan with the pork and then add the fish sauce, lime juice, and simple syrup. Set over medium heat and heat the mixture just until warm to the touch, 15 seconds or so. Turn off the heat.

Add the pork, fungus, tomatoes, white and green onions, and cilantro to the saucepan and toss well. Transfer the salad (including all of the dressing) to a plate in a low heap. Serve right away.

½ teaspoon neutral oil (such as rice bran or canola)

Scant 2 ounces / 50 g ground pork

2 tablespoons Thai fish sauce, plus 2 dashes for the pork

14 g / 4 peeled garlic cloves, halved lengthwise

6 g / 4 stemmed fresh Thai chiles, preferably green

2 tablespoons fresh lime juice, preferably from Key limes or from regular (Persian) limes spiked with a small squeeze of Meyer lemon juice

2 tablespoons Naam Cheuam Naam Taan Piip (Palm sugar simple syrup), page 237

80 g / 1 cup trimmed and coarsely chopped soaked white fungus (see Note)

2 ounces / 55 g cherry tomatoes (about 4 tomatoes), halved, or quartered if very large

30 g / ¼ cup thinly sliced (with the grain) peeled white onion

14 g / ¼ cup very coarsely chopped (about 2 inches / 5 cm) green onions

4 g / 2 tablespoons coarsely chopped cilantro (thin stems and leaves)

TAP WAAN

Isaan pork liver salad ตับหวาน

Like most Thai "salads," this Isaan dish defies the imprecise English translation with its composition—after all, it's mostly pork liver. Those new to the pleasures of this particular organ meat will discover something in between chicken and beef liver, pleasantly firm and relatively mild. Bite-size pieces are poached in water and pulled when they're still slightly pink inside—a striking exception in a country where I've otherwise only seen liver either cooked to hell or eaten raw. Here it's fixed in the Northeastern Thai fashion, subjected to a particularly compelling and fiery combination of lemongrass and lime, dried chiles and toasted-rice powder. ◊ *serves 4*

Bring a pot of water to a boil over high heat, then lower the heat to maintain a very gentle simmer. You're after tiny bubbles that don't break the surface (160°F to 180°F / 71°C to 82°C).

Put the pork liver in the noodle basket.

While the water is heating, combine the lemongrass, lime juice, fish sauce, stock, sugar, and chile powder in a saucepan. Set over medium heat and heat the mixture just until warm to the touch, 15 seconds or so. Turn off the heat.

Dip the noodle basket in the simmering water, submerging the liver fully, and cook, gently shaking the basket constantly to keep the pieces moving around, until the liver is cooked on the outside but still slightly pink in the center, 15 to 20 seconds. Shake the basket to drain well.

Transfer the liver to the saucepan with the lemongrass mixture, add the shallots, mint, cilantro, and rice powder, and toss well. Season to taste with fish sauce and chile powder.

Transfer the salad (including all of the dressing) to a plate in a low heap. Sprinkle on a pinch or so of rice powder and serve right away.

SPECIAL EQUIPMENT
A long-handled noodle basket

---

4 ounces / 115 g pork liver, cut into bite-size slices ¼ inch / 6 mm thick

15 g thinly sliced lemongrass (tender parts only), from about 2 large stalks

1½ tablespoons fresh lime juice, preferably from Key limes or from regular (Persian) limes spiked with a small squeeze of Meyer lemon juice

1½ tablespoons Thai fish sauce

1 tablespoon Sup Kraduuk Muu (Thai pork stock), page 241, or water

4 g / 1 teaspoon granulated sugar

1 g / 1 teaspoon Phrik Pon Khua (Toasted-chile powder), page 233

32 g / ¼ cup thinly sliced (with the grain) peeled Asian shallots

3 g / ¼ cup small mint leaves

8 g / ¼ cup coarsely chopped cilantro (thin stems and leaves)

4 g / 1 heaping teaspoon Khao Khua (Toasted–sticky rice powder), page 232, plus a large pinch for finishing

LAAP NEUA DIP

ลาบเนื้อดิบ   Nan-style minced raw beef "salad"

SPECIAL EQUIPMENT

A granite mortar and pestle

A deep-fry thermometer

A large spider skimmer (recommended)

A solid wooden chopping block (recommended)

A meat cleaver

The most common way to eat *laap meuang*, the minced meat "salad" done in the Northern style, when you're drinking is *dip* (raw). Often the uncooked dish includes not just meat—typically pork, beef, or buffalo—but raw blood and bitter bile as well. To ward off any potentially harmful organisms or bacteria, most seasoned eaters will advise you to eat *laap dip* along with large quantities of the local firewater, *lao khao*. In Nan province, next to the border with Laos, many cooks add a rather sophisticated touch, mixing the raw meat with deep-fried offal and aromatics, like lemongrass and makrut lime leaves. It's a genius move. ◊ *serves 6 to 8*

◊ ◊ ◊

Laap Paste

1 ounce stemmed dried Mexican puya chiles

5 g makhwen

5 g / 1 tablespoon coriander seeds

2 g / 1 teaspoon fennel seeds

1 g / ½ teaspoon ground dried galangal

1 g / ½ teaspoon ground dried lemongrass

1 g / ½ teaspoon black peppercorns

¼ teaspoon cumin seeds

⅛ teaspoon freshly grated nutmeg

4 cloves

2 g / 2 dried long peppers

1 star anise pod

1 whole mace

1 cardamom pod, preferably the white, rounder Thai variety

3 g kosher salt

1 ounce peeled garlic cloves, halved lengthwise

2 ounces thinly sliced (against the grain) peeled Asian shallots

17 g Kapi Kung (Homemade shrimp paste), page 238

Offal

3 ounces / 85 g beef offal (a mixture of liver, heart, and tripe), cut into about 2-inch / 5-cm pieces

3 g / ½ teaspoon Kapi Kung (Homemade shrimp paste), page 238

7 g unpeeled fresh or thawed frozen galangal, coarsely sliced

1 large stalk lemongrass, bottom 1 inch / 2.5 cm, top 9 inches / 23 cm, and outer layer removed, halved crosswise and lightly smashed with a pestle, a pan, or the flat surface of a knife blade

2 cups / 480 ml water

Make the laap paste

Put the puya chiles in a small, dry frying pan or wok, set over high heat until the pan is hot, and then turn down the heat to low. Cook the chiles, stirring and flipping them frequently to make sure both sides of each chile make contact with the hot pan, until they are brittle and very dark brown all over, 15 to 20 minutes. Remove the chiles from the pan as they are ready. (Discard any seeds that escape from the chiles as they will burn and be bitter.) Set the chiles aside.

Combine the makhwen, coriander seeds, fennel seeds, galangal, lemongrass, black peppercorns, cumin seeds, nutmeg, cloves, long peppers, star anise, mace, and cardamom in a small, dry pan. Set over low heat and cook, stirring and tossing often, until very fragrant, 3 to 5 minutes. Turn off the heat and stir for another minute. Transfer to a spice grinder and grind (or pound in the mortar) to a fairly fine powder.

Combine the chiles and salt in the mortar and pound firmly, occasionally stopping to scrape down the sides of the mortar and stirring the mixture once or twice, until you have a fairly fine powder, about 5 minutes. Add the garlic and pound, again occasionally stopping to scrape down the sides of the mortar, until you have a fairly smooth paste, about 2 minutes. Do the same with the shallots. Add the ground spice mixture and pound until it is well incorporated into the paste, about 2 minutes. Finally, add the shrimp paste and pound until fully incorporated, about 30 seconds.

You'll have about 100 g / ½ cup paste. Reserve 25 g / 2 tablespoons for this recipe and store the remainder in an airtight container in the fridge for up to 1 week or in the freezer for up to 6 months.

Cook the offal

Combine the offal, shrimp paste, galangal, lemongrass, and water in a small saucepan, set over high heat, and bring to a strong simmer. Check the pork liver. Once it's cooked through (firm and just barely pink in the center), transfer it to a cutting board. Turn down the heat to maintain a gentle but steady simmer, skimming off any surface scum.

Continue cooking until the heart is fully cooked and the tripe is tender, about 45 minutes. Transfer the heart and tripe to the cutting board with the liver. When all of the offal is cool enough to handle, slice into small bite-size pieces. Pat the offal dry with towels.

Make the dish

Put the Thai chiles in a small, dry frying pan or wok, set over high heat until the pan is hot, and then turn down the heat to low. Cook the chiles, stirring almost constantly and flipping them occasionally, until they are very brittle and dark brown all over, 5 to 8 minutes. Set aside.

Put the beef slices on the chopping block or a heavy cutting board. Use the cleaver or a heavy knife to chop the beef, lifting the knife off the block with each chop and working methodically from one side of the expanse of meat to the other, and then working your way back. Every 15 seconds or so, use the cleaver to scoop up some of the meat and fold it back onto the rest. Keep chopping until the meat is very finely minced (several times finer than store-bought ground meat), about 30 minutes.

Select a heavy pot at least 12 inches / 30 cm wide and pour in the oil to a depth of 2 to 3 inches / 5 to 7.5 cm. Set the pot over high heat and heat the oil to 325°F / 165°C. Use the thermometer to test the temperature, measuring the oil at the center of the vessel and carefully stirring the oil occasionally to ensure a consistent temperature. Line a large sheet pan with paper towels or newspaper and set it near the stove. Add the offal to the hot oil and fry, stirring occasionally, until crunchy, 1 to 2 minutes. Using the spider or a slotted spoon, transfer them to the prepared pan to drain.

Lower the heat to bring the oil to 275°F / 135°C. Add the lemongrass to the hot oil and immediately turn down the heat to low. Cook, stirring occasionally, until crispy and golden brown, about 5 minutes. Using a fine-mesh strainer, transfer the lemongrass to the prepared pan to drain.

Increase the heat to high and wait for a few minutes. Add the lime leaves to the hot oil and cook, stirring occasionally, until crisp but still bright green, about 10 seconds. Using the strainer, transfer the leaves to the pan to drain.

Set a wok or saucepan over medium-low heat, add 2 tablespoons of oil, and swirl the oil in the wok to coat the sides. Add the reserved paste and cook, stirring frequently, until fragrant, 2 to 3 minutes. Turn off the heat, let the mixture cool, and transfer to a bowl.

Add the fish sauce and blood to the bowl and stir well. Add the minced beef, sawtooth herb, green onions, cilantro, and the fried chiles, lemongrass, lime leaves, shallots, and garlic. Mix gently but well and transfer to a plate. Serve right away with the herbs, cabbage, cucumbers, and rice.

For the Dish

6 stemmed dried Thai chiles

Neutral oil (such as soybean or palm), for deep-frying (about 12 cups / 2.8 L)

28 g / ¼ cup thinly sliced lemongrass (tender parts only), from about 4 large stalks

6 g / 10 large fresh or thawed frozen makrut lime leaves, patted dry

8 ounces / 225 g beef tenderloin, cut against the grain into slices about ½ inch / 12 mm thick

2 tablespoons Thai fish sauce

2 tablespoons fresh or thawed frozen raw beef blood (optional)

8 g / ¼ cup thinly sliced sawtooth herb

10 g / 2 tablespoons sliced (¼ inch / 6 mm) green onions

6 g / 3 tablespoons very coarsely chopped cilantro (thin stems and leaves)

20 g / ¼ cup Hom Jiaw (Fried shallots), page 235

15 g / 3 tablespoons Krathiam Jiaw (Fried garlic), page 234

To Serve Alongside

A pile of mixed herbs, such as Vietnamese mint, sawtooth herb, and Thai basil

Several white cabbage wedges

Several thin, crunchy cucumbers, halved lengthwise

Khao Niaw (Sticky rice), page 248

LAAP PHRAE

ลาบแพร่ Phrae-style minced pork "salad"

The martini lunch is alive and well at Jin Sot. But instead of a cocktail and a club sandwich, everyone here drinks beer and eats *laap*.

It's just after noon in Phrae, a town a couple of hours north of Chiang Mai. Phrae is renowned for its *laap*, and Wiwat Kanka's rendition is more than worth the trip. He was born here and runs Jin Sot ("Fresh Meat" in the Northern Thai dialect), a remarkably tidy spot on the road into town. The restaurant's name is apt: I'm digging into a small beet-red pile of raw beef spiked with raw blood, and I'm not dead yet.

Often translated as "ground meat salad," *laap* has two distinct styles and endless variations within them. The style best known in the States hails from Isaan, the Northeast region of Thailand, and features chopped fresh herbs, raw shallots, toasted-rice powder, lime, and dried chiles. I'm better versed in *laap meuang,* the style from the North of Thailand, which trades the bright, fiery thrill of *laap* Isaan for the more complex pleasure of dried spices, such as cumin, coriander, and the seeds of the Northern Thai prickly ash tree called *makhwen*.

The *laap* of the North has a few constants—it always comes with sticky rice and a heap of herbs—but the particulars vary widely. The meat used to make *laap* can be virtually anything, from beef to pork, catfish to chicken, water buffalo to barking deer. (And it isn't ground but rather hacked to a mince, typically with a heavy, machete-like cleaver made specifically for the purpose.) The spice mixture, which is called *naam phrik laap*, might clock in at more than a dozen ingredients or it might contain just a few.

◊ ◊ ◊

When Khun (Mr.) Wiwat was young and dried spices were a relative rarity, his parents made *naam phrik laap* with whatever they could find. These seasonings most likely included an oddity local to Phrae called *ma laep*, the fruits of a local tree that look like dried seeds, taste citrusy, and have a numbing effect on the tongue. Khun Wiwat uses *ma laep* as well as about nine other ingredients, such as long pepper and coriander, in his surprisingly elaborate mixture. In an old-school move, he leaves out shrimp paste, a typical addition to contemporary *naam phrik laap* that likely didn't show up in the *laap* his parents made. A conscientious cook, he makes two different blends—one for *laap* made with pork and the other for *laap* made with beef.

Laap meuang is often cooked—either fried in a dry wok (*laap khua*) or simmered with a little liquid (*laap suk*)—but old-timers are particularly fond of the raw version called *laap dip* and made with beef or water buffalo. So am I. In Phrae, locals prefer their *laap* raw, blood spiked, and bitter from the addition of bile and accompanied by a very spicy raw Chinese mustard green to aid digestion. Here, however, I've shared the recipe for the cooked pork version to avoid offending the delicate sensibilities of my Western readers. And also because it tastes great.

When I'm at a good place like Jin Sot, I don't blink (not anymore, at least) at the thought of eating uncooked bile and blood, though like even the most hardened local, I do reach for a stiff drink. Apprehension certainly isn't the reason the tables here are full of beer bottles. When my culinary mentors were growing up, their families typically reserved *laap* for ceremonies. Meat was a luxury then, and indulging in a dish this heavy on animal flesh required the justification of a special occasion. Since *lao khao* (rice liquor) has long figured heavily in Thai ceremonies, Northern Thais linked up *laap* and booze, a relationship that endures today. *Laap* is not exclusively drinking food—as already noted, few things are—but in Northern Thailand, the places that specialize in it are frequented by *khii mao* (drunkards) more than any other demographic.

Just as you'll probably see people drinking while eating *laap,* you'll also probably notice that in Northern Thailand, *laap dip* is traditionally a man's dish. When you grab a seat at one of the increasingly rare restaurants that specialize in the dish, you'll likely become a member of a predominantly male audience. And it's not just a dish that men tend to eat more often than women do, but one that's most often made by men, too. Even today, when you identify the cook at a *laap* restaurant, nine times out of ten, it's a guy like Khun Wiwat.

He's pleased when my dining buddies and I praise his food. He smiles when we show up the next afternoon to grab a bite on our way out of town. He's proud of his food but shows no signs of ego. When I ask him why everyone around us is drinking while enjoying his *laap,* he laughs and says, "Because that makes it taste better."

◊ *serves 6 to 8*

Note on Ma Laep: No self-respecting *laap* master from Phrae would make the dish without *ma laep*. Since I'd wager you're not one, you can leave it out without utter disaster, since it is more or less impossible to find in the U.S. If you're up for a challenge, however, ask around: You might identify a friend of a friend who'd be willing to bring some back from Northern Thailand.

Make the laap paste

Combine the makhwen, long peppers, and ma laep in the mortar and pound to a fairly fine powder, about 3 minutes.

Add the galangal and salt and pound firmly, scraping the mortar and stirring the mixture once or twice, until you have a fairly fine paste, about 3 minutes. Add the lemongrass and pound, occasionally stopping to scrape down the sides of the mortar, to a fairly smooth paste, about 3 minutes. Do the same with the garlic and then the shallots. Add the chile powder and gently pound until well combined.

You'll have about 140 g / 1 cup paste. You can use it right away, or you can store it in an airtight container in the fridge for up to 1 week or in the freezer for up to 6 months. Reserve 2 tablespoons for this recipe.

A Thai granite mortar and pestle

A solid wooden chopping block (recommended)

A meat cleaver

Laap Paste

14 g makhwen

2 g dried Indonesian long peppers

3 g ma laep (see Note)

27 g peeled fresh or thawed frozen galangal, thinly sliced against the grain

9 g kosher salt

15 g thinly sliced lemongrass (tender parts only), from about 2 large stalks

20 g peeled garlic cloves, halved lengthwise

38 g thinly sliced (against the grain) peeled Asian shallots

6 g Phrik Pon Khua (Toasted-chile powder), page 233

Offal

1 large stalk lemongrass, bottom 1 inch / 2.5 cm, top 9 inches / 23 cm, and outer layer removed

1 ounce / 30 g pork small intestine

1 ounce / 30 g pork skin

1 ounce / 30 g pork liver

3 g / ½ teaspoon Kapi Kung (Homemade shrimp paste), page 238

7 g unpeeled fresh or thawed frozen galangal, coarsely sliced

2 cups / 480 ml water

(continued)

◊ ◊ ◊

Cook the offal

Halve the lemongrass crosswise, and lightly smash it with a pestle, a pan, or the flat surface of a knife blade. Combine the intestine, skin, liver, shrimp paste, galangal, lemongrass, and water in a small saucepan, set over high heat, and bring to a strong simmer. Check the pork liver. Once it's cooked through (firm and just barely pink in the center), transfer it to a cutting board. Turn down the heat to maintain a gentle but steady simmer, skimming off any surface scum.

Continue cooking until the skin is translucent and soft enough to slice easily, about 20 minutes. Transfer the intestine and skin to the cutting board with the liver. When all of the offal is cool enough to handle, slice the intestine and liver into small bite-size pieces. Slice the skin into thin strips 2 inches / 5 cm long.

Make the dish

Put the pork slices on the chopping block or a cutting board. Use a cleaver or a heavy knife to chop the pork, lifting the knife off the block with each chop and working methodically from one side of the expanse of meat to the other, and then working your way back. Every 15 seconds or so, use the cleaver to scoop up some of the meat and fold it back onto the rest. Keep chopping until the meat is very finely minced (several times finer than store-bought ground meat), about 30 minutes.

Combine ½ cup / 120 ml of the stock and the reserved 18 g / 2 table-spoons of paste in a bowl and stir to combine. Add the offal, pork, fried garlic, fish sauce, mint, cilantro, sawtooth herb, and green onions and mix well.

Heat a large frying pan or wok over medium heat, add the garlic oil, and swirl the oil in the pan to coat the sides. Add the meat mixture and cook, stirring constantly and breaking up any clumps, for 1 minute. Add the remaining ¼ cup / 60 ml stock and boil, stirring, until the meat is fully cooked and the liquid has nearly evaporated, about 7 to 8 minutes. Season to taste with fish sauce.

Transfer to a plate and sprinkle with the cracklings and then finish with the fried garlic. Serve right away with the herbs, cabbage, cucumbers, and rice.

For the Dish

8 ounces / 225 g boneless pork loin (without fat cap), cut against the grain into slices about ½ inch / 12 mm thick

¾ cup / 180 ml Sup Kraduuk Muu (Thai pork stock), page 241

10 g / 2 tablespoons Krathiam Jiaw (Fried garlic), page 234, plus large pinch for finishing

Scant 2 teaspoons Thai fish sauce

4 g / 2 tablespoons coarsely chopped Vietnamese mint leaves (rau răm)

4 g / 2 tablespoons coarsely chopped cilantro (thin stems and leaves), plus large pinch for finishing

4 g / 2 tablespoons thinly sliced sawtooth herb, plus large pinch for finishing

4 g / 2 tablespoons sliced (¼ inch / 6 mm) green onions, plus large pinch for finishing

2 teaspoons Naam Man Krathiam (Fried garlic oil), page 234, or Naam Man Hom Jiaw (Fried shallot oil), page 235

5 g / 2 tablespoons very coarsely crumbled pork cracklings, homemade (page 107) or store-bought

To Serve Alongside

A pile of mixed herbs, such as Vietnamese mint, sawtooth herb, and Thai basil

Several white cabbage wedges

Several thin, crunchy cucumbers, halved lengthwise

Khao Niaw (Sticky rice), page 248

KHAWNG PHAT
STIR-FRIES
ของผัด

A NOTE ON STIR-FRYING

The stir-fry recipes in this book were developed using a carbon-steel wok and a gas stove-top burner turned up as high as it can go. Even without the jet-burner-like heat required by the classic Chinese technique, the process goes quickly, so it's important to be organized. Prep and measure all of the ingredients before you even turn on the heat.

To stir-fry, use a wok spatula to push, scoop, and flip the ingredients more or less the whole time. As you work, keep in mind the purpose of the technique: to cook the ingredients relatively briefly. You need to stir constantly to ensure all of the ingredients make plenty of contact with the hot surface and don't have a chance to burn or stick. It's also important to scrape the bottom of the pan occasionally as you stir.

If you're cursed with an electric burner, consider using a cast-iron wok. It holds heat far better than a thin steel or aluminum wok, which helps combat the main problem with stir-frying on an electric burner: when you add a bunch of ingredients to the wok, not only will the wok itself cool down, but the heating element will, too. Be aware that cooking times provided in the recipes will be different if you're using a heavy wok.

PHAT KHII MAO

Drunkard's stir-fry   ผัดขี้เมา

Way back in 2013, while I was in the throes of researching this book, I approached Anthony Bourdain and asked if he'd consider meeting up in Thailand to share a drink or two at a spot that specialized in *aahaan kap klaem*. To my surprise, he proposed devoting an episode of his CNN show *Parts Unknown* to the drinking food of Thailand. I eagerly volunteered to be his guide. This, I figured, was the perfect opportunity for my first foray into *phat khii mao*.

After all, of all of Thailand's drinking food, *phat khii mao* is perhaps the only dish named for its purpose. The literal translation is "drunkard's stir-fry." The explanations for this title vary. Some say a drunk man invented the dish, his hunger inspiring its late-night, raid-the-fridge composition—just as my buddy Adam (who edited the photos in this book) and I, as pissed lads, used to throw together pasta, peanut butter, celery, and chile that we found when we raided his roommate's fridge late at night. Others claim the name comes from the aggressive seasoning meant to tear through the dulled palates of the inebriated. Whatever the reason, *phat khii mao* became quintessential boozer grub—fiery and salty enough to encourage another round.

Americans might not know much Thai, but my guess is that if you're reading this book, you have at some point rattled off the words *pad kee mao*. Like *phat thai* and green curry, *phat khii mao* (as I prefer to transliterate the dish's name) is so ubiquitous on Thai menus in the United States that you'd think you'd find it on every street

◇ ◇ ◇

A Thai granite mortar
and pestle

An 11- to 14-inch flat-
bottomed aluminum,
stainless steel, or carbon
steel wok

A wok spatula

corner in Thailand. Yet during more than two decades of eating in Thailand, the dish never made it onto my table—not abroad or in the States. I had nothing against it. But in Thailand, at least outside of the tourist ghettos, *phat khii mao* is just one Central Thai dish among hundreds. There was so much else to try. The story was similar back home, where I typically seek out a Thai restaurant's specialty—that is, what Thai customers order. And that's just never happened to be *phat khii mao*.

I might not have eaten *phat khii mao*, but I was aware of its defining ingredient: noodles. Nearly every American menu offers the translation "drunken noodles." In Thailand, I've seen the dish in woks and on tables, and it featured noodles as well. This struck me as odd, since I kept hearing from knowledgeable friends in Thailand that the original dish didn't contain noodles. By now, I'm used to these seemingly contradictory revelations—constant reminders of the chasm between our understanding of "Thai food" and the food of Thailand.

To get some answers and to make sure Tony ate well, I put out the word among friends that I was looking for a place that served a killer version of the noodle-less dish. I settled on Raan Kaphrao Samrap Khon Chawp Kin Phet, or "Restaurant That Sells Stir-Fried Holy Basil Dishes for People Who Like to Eat Spicy Food." (No shit, that's more or less the name.) It isn't frequented only by the intoxicated, but it does attract its fair share. When a waitress, surprised to see a group of *farang* enter (me, Bourdain, and a camera crew, no less), asked which of us had picked the restaurant, someone nodded in my direction. She smiled and asked, teasingly, "*Pen khii mao, chai mai?*"—"He's a drunkard, right?"

Since that visit, I've been haunting the restaurant to eat its exemplary version of *phat khii mao* as well as several other spicy classics and to interrogate the owner, Mae Tu.

Even in Thailand, *phat khii mao* has become so closely associated with noodles that many people assume it is and always has been a noodle dish. Mae Tu is not one of these people. "The original was not," she said. "But nowadays, Thai people want to eat everything with noodles." Sometimes the evolution of food involves immigration, occupation, and war. In this case, I suspect it's just because Thai people love noodles. In an ironic twist of cultural crossbreeding, if you conduct an Internet search in Thai for *phat khii mao*, the top hit is "spaghetti *khii mao*"—aka the dish made not with wide rice noodles but with spaghetti.

To come up with her rendition, Mae Tu ate the dish all over, then came up with a composite that showcased her favorite qualities (essentially what I try to do at my restaurants), in particular several sources of aroma and heat: *phrik khii nuu* (rat-shit chiles) crushed with garlic, *phrik thai awn* (fresh green peppercorns), *bai kaphrao* (holy basil), *krachai* (a spindly ginger relative), and slivers of *phrik chii faa* (skyward pointing chiles). These strike a beautiful balance in the saucy, noodle-less jumble of beef, long bean, baby corn, and onion. To those raised on the starchy American version, Mae Tu's take is only vaguely recognizable.

Although no rigid formula exists for any food, and particularly not for a dish thought to be concocted on the fly by a sot, there are emblematic seasonings. "You can't forget the green peppercorns or the *krachai*," she told me, which of course, American versions almost always do, perhaps because in America these ingredients, at least until recently, have been almost impossible to find fresh.

She doesn't explicitly offer *phat khii mao* with noodles, though she doesn't deny the occasional customer who requests it. So much of the food in Thailand, especially dishes made to order such as stir-fries and papaya salad, is customizable. This makes it especially susceptible to shifting tastes and fashions, even changes to its fundamental makeup. The noodle version, then, has become as Thai as anything. Still, when I'm crowded around a table full of beer, it's the original *phat khii mao* that gets my attention. It's the dish that sent Tony Bourdain into a fever dream. Mae Tu was proud. To this day, she displays a banner with a photo of her and her family with Tony at the front of the restaurant.

◊ *serves 4*

◊ ◊ ◊

14 g / 4 peeled garlic cloves, halved lengthwise

6 g / 4 stemmed fresh red Thai chiles

8 g / 1 tablespoon fresh or drained pickled green peppercorns, in bunches 1 inch / 2.5 cm long

8 g / 2 tablespoons thawed frozen preshredded krachai (Chinese keys)

6 g / 2 tablespoons thinly sliced (⅛ inch / 3 mm) moderately spicy fresh long green chiles (such as goat horn or Hungarian wax)

6 g / 2 tablespoons thinly sliced (⅛ inch / 3 mm) moderately spicy fresh long red chiles (such as Fresno)

3 g / 2 stemmed fresh green Thai chiles, bruised

1 tablespoon Thai oyster sauce

1 teaspoon Thai fish sauce

1 teaspoon Thai thin soy sauce

1 teaspoon rice liquor (such as Shaoxing wine or shochu)

1 g / ¼ teaspoon granulated sugar

2 tablespoons rice oil, soybean oil, or rendered pork fat

3 ounces / 85 g boneless flank steak, beef chuck flap, or wild boar shoulder, cut into slices 2 by ¾ by ⅛ inch / 5 cm by 2 cm by 3 mm

40 g / ⅓ cup thinly sliced (with the grain) peeled yellow onion

40 g / ⅓ cup long beans, trimmed and cut into 1½-inch / 4-cm lengths

30 g / ½ cup fresh or thawed frozen baby corn, halved lengthwise

¼ cup plus 2 tablespoons / 90 ml Sup Kraduuk Muu (Thai pork stock), page 241, or water

12 g / ½ cup holy basil (bai kaphrao) leaves

Prep the dish

Combine the garlic and red Thai chiles in the mortar and pound just until the garlic is in small pieces and you have a slightly wet-looking mixture (not a paste), about 15 seconds. Set aside 12 g / 1 tablespoon for this dish. Reserve the remainder for another purpose.

Combine the peppercorns, *krachai*, long green chiles, long red chiles, and bruised green Thai chiles in a small bowl. In a separate small bowl, combine the oyster sauce, fish sauce, soy sauce, liquor, and sugar and stir until the sugar dissolves.

Cook the dish

Heat the wok over medium heat, add the oil, and swirl the oil to coat the sides of the wok. When the oil smokes lightly, add the garlic-chile mixture and remove the wok from the heat. Cook off the heat, stirring constantly and quickly, until the mixture is fragrant but has not taken on color, 30 seconds to 1 minute. Do yourself a favor and avoid taking too deep or too close a sniff.

Put the wok back on the heat, turn the heat as high as it will go, and add the meat. Stir-fry (constantly stir, scoop, and flip the ingredients) for 30 seconds. Add the peppercorn-chile mixture and stir-fry for 30 seconds. Add the onion, long beans, and baby corn and stir-fry for 15 seconds. Add the oyster sauce mixture, stir well, and then add the stock. Stir-fry until the liquid comes to a boil, about 30 seconds. Turn off the heat, immediately add the basil, and stir well.

Transfer to a plate and serve right away.

KHUA HAEM PIK KAI

Stir-fried chicken wings
with hot basil and chiles

คั่วแฮ่มปีกไก่

I've been eating in Thailand for a long time, yet I still
approach every trip as a chance to learn something
new. Any restaurant recommendation from a good cook
gets scribbled down. Any lead from a clued-in friend is
dutifully followed. That's how I ended up sucking on
bone, sinew, and cartilage at a karaoke joint in the town
of Mae Rim.

I had gotten a tip from Chai Cha Tri, an old friend
and former *muay thai* champion with a face sculpted by
fists and feet. He is very much a man of the rural North.
He still lives a short walk from where he grew up, in the
village of Saluang Nai. His first language is Northern Thai
dialect (he speaks rudimentary English and rough Thai).
The son of Da Chom, the man who originally taught me
to make *laap*, Tri was raised on the sorts of foods that
I discovered late in life and transformed my life to pursue.
He is as eager to send me to potentially illuminating
dining experiences as he is to warn me off sketchy ones.
As we drive the twisting byways outside Chiang Mai, he'll
often point out a bar and say, in halting, heavily accented
English: "Bad. People. Here."

There were no bad people at Laap Plaa Pia Nong Haw,
where Tri sent me one night—or none that I could identify
anyway. I was too busy eating. Thanks to Tri, I had come
upon a dish here I'd never tried before: *khua haem*. The
dish struck me as a sort of Northern Thai version of *Phat
Khii Mao* ("Drunkard's stir-fry"), page 201: a salty, fragrant,

◊ ◊ ◊

wickedly spicy stir-fry of chiles, hot basil, and, in this case, hacked-up chicken wings. Eating it requires the kind of gnawing, chewing, and frequent brow dabbing common to many of the finest examples of *aahaan kap klaem*.

Yet when I asked around about *khua haem*, my girlfriend, Kung, told me that her mother used to make it for the family at their home in Chiang Kong, a town near the Thai border with Laos. Her parents were rice farmers. Her mother made the dish with whatever meat, bones, and bits she could get her hands on and gathered the rest of the ingredients from what plants grew in the village. The dish ain't palace food. It reflects resourcefulness born of poverty, not of privilege. It's an example of lowly ingredients made exciting. Kung's family ate it for dinner with other dishes like *naam phrik, kaeng awm neua* (Northern Thai stewed beef), and sticky rice. Context matters, and *khua haem* isn't exclusively food for boozing. But when the liquor is flowing and a blotto rice farmer is serenading you with melancholy *lukthung* songs, the dish takes on a different purpose and few things are better.

The word *khua* in the name of this dish basically means "dry fried" and suggests that this version, like most that I've eaten, is stir-fried until any liquid in the wok is gone. Yet occasionally, the dish ends up saucier, as it appears in the photo you see opposite. If you want yours slightly saucy, add ½ cup / 120 ml water to the wok just before you take it off the heat. ◊ ***serves 4 to 6***

◊ ◊ ◊

A Thai granite mortar and pestle

An 11- to 14-inch flat-bottomed aluminum, stainless steel, or carbon steel wok

A wok spatula

A lid large enough to cover the wok

2¼ pounds / 1 kg chicken wing flats and drumettes

2 tablespoons Thai fish sauce

3 g / 1 teaspoon kosher salt

1 large stalk lemongrass, bottom 1 inch / 2.5 cm, top 9 inches / 23 cm, and outer layer removed

5 g / 5 cilantro roots

3 g / 5 stemmed dried Thai chiles

3 g / 1 teaspoon black peppercorns

28 g / 9 peeled garlic cloves, halved lengthwise

12 g / 8 stemmed fresh red Thai chiles

3 g / 4 large fresh or frozen makrut lime leaves

½ cup / 120 ml neutral oil (such as rice bran or canola)

1½ cups / 360 ml water

1 tablespoon Thai thin soy sauce

48 g / 2 cups holy basil (bai kaphrao) leaves or fresh cumin leaves

Marinate the chicken

Put the wings in a large bowl, add the fish sauce and salt, and toss to coat well. Cover and marinate at room temperature for at least 30 minutes or up to 1 hour.

Make the dish

Cut the lemongrass crosswise into 1-inch / 2.5-cm lengths. Combine the cilantro roots, dried chiles, and peppercorns in the mortar and pound to a coarse paste, about 20 seconds. Add the garlic and fresh chiles and pound to a very coarse paste, about 20 seconds. Remove the chicken wings from the marinade and discard the marinade. Add the lemongrass and lime leaves and briefly pound to crush and release their oils, about 10 seconds. Set the mixture aside.

Heat the oil in the wok over high heat until it begins to smoke and then swirl the oil to coat the sides of the wok. Add the chicken wings and cook, stirring and flipping occasionally, until they are more or less browned all over, about 5 minutes.

Drain off the oil and reserve 2 tablespoons. Add 1 cup / 240 ml of the water, turn down the heat to medium, and cover the wok with the lid. Cook at a rapid simmer for 5 minutes, then remove the lid, turn up the heat to high, and cook, stirring and flipping the chicken occasionally, until all of the liquid has evaporated, about 10 minutes.

Push the chicken to one side of the wok. Add the reserved 2 tablespoons oil to the empty space and let it smoke lightly. Add the lemongrass mixture to the oil, then stir-fry with the chicken (constantly stir, scoop, and flip the ingredients) for about 30 seconds.

Add the soy sauce and stir-fry for 1 minute. Add the remaining ½ cup / 120 ml water and continue stir-frying until the liquid has evaporated and the lemongrass mixture starts to stick to the wok, 1 to 2 minutes more.

Remove the wok from the heat and let cool slightly, about 3 minutes. Add the basil or cumin leaves and toss well.

Transfer to a plate, scraping to get at the flavorful stuff stuck to the wok, and serve right away.

PHAT HOI LAAI SAMUN PHRAI

Stir-fried clams with krachai, galangal, and Thai basil

ผัดหอยลายสมุนไพร

Typically, I spend my time first ferreting out some great version of an herbaceous soup or fiery jumble of flesh and then figuring out how to faithfully re-create it. Occasionally I'll have to identify stand-ins for ingredients I can't get in the States, or I'll piece together a composite of a few of my favorite versions, but that's about as close to employing creativity as I get.

This dish represents a rare departure. I've eaten many stir-fried clams in Thailand, most often spiked with the slightly sticky paste called *naam phrik phao* that gives the dish its flavor profile—sweet from palm sugar, funky from some preserved shrimp product, and hot from chiles. But I prefer this version, constructed not from the memories of empty plates but from reading the limited but fascinating English-language literature on the food of Thailand. (That I don't read Thai is a longtime source of shame.) I get particularly geeked out on the food column Suthon Sukphisit writes for the *Bangkok Post,* where I first found mention of something resembling this preparation. More reading and some experimenting led me to what I think would cause no sneers on tables in Thailand: briny clams in a vibrant broth headlined by a highly aromatic combination of fresh chiles, Thai basil, and *krachai,* a spindly rhizome with an earthy, peppery flavor.

◊ ◊ ◊

The tiny bivalves used in Thailand—the word *laai* in the name of the dish refers to the cool crosshatched pattern on their shells—are worth seeking out, but Manila clams or cockles work well. Since I'm playing fast and loose anyway, I bet even mussels would do.

◊ *serves 4 to 6*

Firmly tap the shells of any open clams. If they don't close by themselves, they're dead and should be discarded.

Combine the water and salt in a bowl and stir until the salt dissolves. Stir in the cornmeal, add the clams, and then add the ice. Let the clams sit for 1 hour to purge the sand from inside their shells. Drain and rinse well.

Combine the garlic and chiles in the mortar and pound just until the garlic is in small pieces and you have a slightly wet-looking mixture (not a paste), about 15 seconds. Set aside 12 g / 1 tablespoon for the dish. Reserve the remainder for another use.

Heat the wok over medium heat, add the oil, and swirl the oil to coat the sides of the wok. When the oil shimmers, add the chile-garlic mixture, galangal, and *krachai* and remove the wok from the heat. Cook off the heat, stirring constantly and quickly, until the mixture is fragrant but has not taken on color, 30 seconds to 1 minute. Do yourself a favor and avoid taking too deep or too close a sniff.

Put the wok back on the heat, turn the heat to high, add the clams and fish sauce, and cook, stirring constantly, for 1 minute. Add the stock, lime juice, and sugar, stir well, and cover the wok with the lid. Cook, shaking the wok occasionally, until the clams open, about 3 minutes.

Turn off the heat, add the basil leaves, and toss well.

Transfer to a bowl. Sprinkle on the green onions and serve right away.

SPECIAL EQUIPMENT

A Thai granite mortar and pestle

An 11- to 14-inch flat-bottomed aluminum, stainless steel, or carbon steel wok

A wok spatula

A lid large enough to cover the wok

1 pound / 455 g Manila clams, littleneck clams, or cockles, scrubbed

12 cups / 2.8 L water

45 g / 5 tablespoons kosher salt

About 3 g / 1 teaspoon cornmeal

225 g / 1 cup ice

14 g / 4 peeled garlic cloves, halved lengthwise

6 g / 4 stemmed fresh Thai chiles, preferably red, thinly sliced

2 tablespoons neutral oil (such as rice bran or canola)

6 g / 1 tablespoon peeled fresh or thawed frozen galangal cut into matchsticks about 2 by ⅛ inch / 5 cm by 3 mm

2 g / 1 teaspoon thawed frozen preshredded krachai (Chinese keys)

1 tablespoon Thai fish sauce

¾ cup / 180 ml Sup Kraduuk Muu (Thai pork stock), page 241, or water

2 tablespoons fresh lime juice, preferably from Key limes or from regular (Persian) limes spiked with a small squeeze of Meyer lemon juice

4 g / 1 teaspoon granulated sugar

12 g / ½ cup Thai basil leaves

5 g / 1 tablespoon sliced (¼ inch / 6 mm) green onions

Khawng Phat: Stir-Fries

KHAWNG KIN RAWP DEUK / KHAWNG KIN CHAO

LATE-NIGHT AND MORNING FOOD

ของกินรอบดึก / เช้า

KHAO TOM

ข้าวต้ม   Rice soup

Khao tom means "boiled rice" in Thai. It might not seem like something you'd seek out in a country known for its fiery curries and lime-spiked salads. But then one night you get truly hammered and some wise soul leads you toward a bowl.

There are generally two kinds of *khao tom*, both equally compelling. One is the sort you'd find at Khao Tom Jay Suay, on a fragrant side street just off one of Bangkok Chinatown's raucous main drags, or at Khao Tom Patom, a cavernous restaurant in Chiang Mai with all of the charm of an airplane hangar. At places like these, *khao tom* isn't the main attraction. It's a porridge—plain, starchy, and filling—that arrives in small bowls to accompany a variety of dishes of Chinese origin: perhaps *jap chai* (soupy stewed mustard greens with a few hunks of pork), stir-fried *phak krachet* (water mimosa), or pig's ear stewed with five spice.

Then there's the kind of *khao tom* featured here, which is more of a rice soup than a porridge, rich from pork stock and coddled egg and seasoned with fish sauce, salted radish, herbs, and aromatic garlic oil. No dishes come along with it, but like its bland counterpart, it soaks up booze so you can begin to feel like yourself again. ◊ ***serves 4***

Note on Pork Balls: Instead of the pork balls, you can substitute 16 peeled medium-size shrimp or 8 ounces / 225 g white-fleshed fish fillets, cut into slices ¼ inch / 6 mm thick.

Combine the stock, soy sauce, fish sauce, radish, and pepper in a saucepan. Add the rice and pork balls (or shrimp or fish, see Note, below) and stir gently. Bring the stock to a boil over medium-high heat, then immediately add the rice. Let the liquid come back to a boil and cook, stirring occasionally, until the rice is hot and the pork balls are heated through or the shrimp or fish is cooked through, 2 to 3 minutes.

Pour the soup into individual bowls. Crack an egg into each bowl, then top with the celery, cilantro, green onions, garlic, and garlic oil. Serve right away.

8 cups / 2 L Sup Kraduuk Muu (Thai pork stock), page 241

¼ cup / 60 ml Thai thin soy sauce

¼ cup / 60 ml Thai fish sauce

14 g / 1½ tablespoons shredded Thai salted radish, soaked in cold water for 10 minutes, then drained well

Ground white pepper (from an Asian market)

455 g / 4 cups Khao Hom Mali (Jasmine rice), page 247, preferably a day or two old

32 Muu Deng (Bouncy pork balls), page 246 (about 8 ounces / 225 g), see Note

4 soft-poached eggs (optional but recommended); see Note, page 218

6 g / ¼ cup coarsely chopped Chinese celery (thin stems and leaves)

8 g / ¼ cup coarsely chopped cilantro (thin stems and leaves)

20 g / ¼ cup sliced (¼ inch / 6 mm) green onions

10 g / 2 tablespoons Krathiam Jiaw (Fried garlic), page 234

2 tablespoons Naam Man Krathiam (Fried garlic oil), page 234

Khawng Kin Rawp Deuk / Khawng Kin Chao: Late-Night and Morning Food

JOK

Rice porridge   โจ๊ก

Jok Ton Phayom serves what is currently my favorite version of *jok* in Chiang Mai. The place sells out by the time most travelers are finishing their morning coffee. From 5:00 a.m., it's packed with a sundry crowd typical at restaurants that specialize in this rice porridge: some are up in time to give daily offerings to monks or to grab breakfast before work at a nearby market. These chronic early risers sit tits to elbows with haggard carousers and gamblers who haven't yet been to bed.

When I first stumbled in one morning a few years back, Jok Ton Phayom had already enjoyed decades of distinction. Just as the walls of a venerable Italian restaurant in New York might be plastered with signed photos of Robert De Niro and Jackie Gleason, here the walls are covered with framed snapshots of Thai actors, as well as of a celebrity forensic scientist famous for her Goth look. Up front is an open kitchen cluttered with *mise en place*, where two busy men in aprons and baseball caps ladle an unassuming white mush from a cauldron into pink bowls and directly into to-go bags.

This mush is *jok*, essentially rice porridge done Thai style, similar to but more flavorful than Chinese congee. Cooks simmer rice until it breaks down to become a tasty sludge. (Lesser restaurants substitute a sort of Cream of Wheat for real rice.) That's basically it, besides some ginger slivers, sliced green onions, a coddled egg, and perhaps a few misshapen pork meatballs. In the morning, it's just the ticket, along with plenty of self-serve white pepper and maybe a few dashes of Maggi, a dark liquid form of MSG. It's just the thing to rescue the hungover, to pull you back from the precipice. ◊ *serves 4*

◊ ◊ ◊

A deep-fry thermometer

A large spider skimmer
(recommended)

Noodle Garnish (Optional)

Neutral oil (such as
soybean or palm), for
deep-frying (about
5 cups / 1.2 L)

16 g / ¼ cup very thin
dried rice vermicelli
noodles (sen mii in Thai)

Porridge

12 cups / 2.8 L water

360 g / 1½ cups broken
Thai jasmine rice

2 cups / 480 ml Sup
Kraduuk Muu (Thai pork
stock), page 241

¼ cup / 60 ml Thai thin
soy sauce

14 g / 1½ tablespoons
shredded Thai salted
radish, soaked in cold
water for 10 minutes,
then drained well

Ground white pepper
(from an Asian market)

32 Muu Deng (Bouncy pork
balls), page 246 (about
8 ounces / 225 g); see Note

40 g / ½ cup very
finely julienned
peeled fresh ginger

20 g / ¼ cup sliced
(¼ inch / 6 mm)
green onions

4 soft-poached
eggs (optional but
recommended),
see Note

Note on Pork Balls: Instead of the pork balls, you can substitute 16 peeled medium-size shrimp or 8 ounces / 225 g white-fleshed fish fillets, cut into slices ¼ inch / 6 mm thick.

Fry the noodle garnish

Pour the oil to a depth of 1½ inches / 4 cm into a heavy pot or wok, set over high heat, and heat the oil to 390°F / 199°C. Use the thermometer to test the temperature, measuring the oil at the center of the vessel and carefully stirring the oil occasionally to ensure a consistent temperature. Line a plate with paper towels or newspaper and set it near the stove.

Add the noodles to the hot oil and fry just until puffed and crispy, about 5 seconds. Using the spider or a large slotted spoon, transfer them to the prepared plate to drain.

Make and serve the porridge

Bring the water to a boil in a saucepan over high heat. Add the rice, adjust the heat to maintain a simmer, and cook, stirring frequently, until the rice breaks down to form a thick porridge that resembles cooked coarse grits, about 1 hour. Remove all but 6 cups of the porridge, reserving the rest for another time.

Add the stock, soy sauce, radish, and several shakes of pepper to the rice mixture and stir well. Add the pork balls (or the shrimp or fish, see Note, below) and stir gently. Raise the heat to medium-high and bring the mixture to a boil. Cook, stirring constantly, until the porridge is glossy and the pork balls are heated through or the shrimp or fish is cooked through, 2 to 3 minutes.

Pour the porridge into individual bowls and divide the ginger and green onions among them. Crack an egg into each bowl, then top with about one-fourth of the noodles. Serve right away.

Note on Making Soft-Poached Eggs for *Jok* and *Khao Tom* (hat tip to David Chang): Pour 6 quarts of water into a pot, clip a deep-fry thermometer to the side of the pot so the prong is in the center of the vessel, and bring the water to 155°F / 70°C over medium heat. Make a ring out of aluminum foil to line the bottom of the pot, and rest a heatproof bowl on top. Carefully add the eggs, reduce the heat to low, and set a timer for 45 minutes. Cook, adjusting the heat or adding a few ice cubes as necessary, to maintain 140°F / 60°C. When the timer goes off, transfer the eggs to a big bowl of ice water until cool. They'll keep at room temperature for up to 4 hours. When you're ready to serve, carefully crack the eggs directly into the bowls of *jok* or *khao tom*.

TOM LEUAT MUU

Pork soup with steamed blood cakes and offal

ต้มเลือดหมู

Jok restaurants don't have big menus. They're focused on early-morning operations that sell just a handful of dishes: the headlining rice porridge, of course, and maybe toast stained yellow with margarine, coddled eggs, and *patangko*, deep-fried crullers for dipping into hot soymilk. They sell coffee, and if you're lucky, it's made the old way, brewed in a strainer that's long and slack like a sock.

And if you're really lucky, they'll offer *tom leuat muu*, a salty pork broth with innards like liver and intestines, slices of blood cake, and a small tangle of greens thrown in for good measure. Alongside, you might get a small bowl of *naam jim*, a tart, salty, spicy dipping sauce for the offal. This is fortifying food, the type of thing you want, even if you don't know it, after a hard night. ◊ *serves 4*

Note on Blood Cakes: Steamed blood (sometimes labeled blood cake) ends up in chunks floating in some soups and curries. It is sold in blocks in the butcher case or refrigerated section at Chinese and other Asian markets.

◊ ◊ ◊

Cook the offal

Lightly smash the lemongrass with a pestle, a pan, or the flat surface of a knife blade, then cut crosswise into 1-inch / 2.5-cm pieces.

Combine the lemongrass, offal (but not the liver), fish sauce, galangal, peppercorns, and water in a small pot. Set the pot over high heat and bring the water to a strong simmer. Cover, adjust the heat to maintain a steady simmer, and cook, occasionally stirring and skimming off any surface scum, until the offal is tender, about 1 hour. About 5 minutes before the offal is ready, add the liver and simmer until firm and just barely pink in the center. Using a slotted spoon, transfer the offal to a cutting board and cut into bite-size pieces. Discard the cooking liquid.

Make and serve the soup

Divide the ribs, offal, and blood cake, and pork balls among 4 wide soup bowls. Add one-fourth each of the mugwort, soy sauce, and pepper to each bowl. Pour 1 cup / 240 ml of the hot broth over the contents of each bowl and sprinkle on the green onions and cilantro.

Serve right away with more soy sauce, pepper, and chile powder on the side.

Offal

1 large stalk lemongrass, bottom 1 inch / 2.5 cm, top 9 inches / 23 cm, and outer layer removed

Scant 8 ounces / 200 g mixed pork offal (such as tendon, tripe, skin, intestine, liver, spleen, and heart)

2 tablespoons Thai fish sauce

25 g / 3 tablespoons thinly sliced peeled fresh or thawed frozen galangal

9 g / 1 tablespoon white peppercorns (from an Asian market)

8 cups / 2 L water

Soup

4 cups / 960 ml Sup Kraduuk Muu (Thai pork stock), including 8 ribs, page 241, hot

3½ ounces / 100 g pork blood cake (see Note, page 219), cut into bite-size pieces

28 g / 1 cup fresh mugwort or epazote leaves (optional)

2 tablespoons plus 2 teaspoons Thai thin soy sauce, plus more for serving

3 g / 1 teaspoon ground white pepper (from an Asian market), plus more for serving

10 g / 2 tablespoons sliced (¼ inch / 6 mm) green onions

4 g / 2 tablespoons coarsely chopped cilantro (thin stems and leaves)

Phrik Pon Khua (Toasted-chile powder), page 233, for serving

KUAYTIAW LUUK CHIN PLAA HUA NOM

Noodle soup with
tiny fish balls

ก๋วยเตี๋ยวลูกชิ้นปลาหัวนม

The fish ball noodle soup is the second most famous
thing about Ong Tipparot, a popular late-night spot in
Chiang Mai. Above the din, where being a bit merry
seems like a condition for entry, you can hear a rapid-fire
drone of a young waiter, as he tabulates orders out loud.
His talent (and distinctive drone) is so well-known that
one of Thailand's most famous stand-up comedians has
devoted a bit to the guy.

The reputation of the restaurant's signature soup
is worthy, too. Each order brings a barely embellished
bowl of broth, your choice of noodles, and spheres of
fish, fat, and flour that, unlike the standard-issue balls,
actually taste of the sea. Also, unlike the typical balls, the
ones here are especially small, hence their crude moniker
around town: *hua nom* (nipple).

This is solid postdrinking fare: simple, salty, and
invigorating, plus there's nothing in it to break your teeth
on. The soup comes in the kind of moderate portion that's
typical in Thailand, so sometimes I take down a second
bowl. I'll often order the similarly restorative pork bone

◊ ◊ ◊

Bowl

2 green-leaf lettuce leaves

1 tablespoon Thai fish sauce

4 g / 1 teaspoon granulated sugar

Less than 1 g / ⅛ teaspoon ground white pepper (from an Asian market)

Soup

2½ ounces / 70 g semidried thin, flat rice noodles (about 2 cups)

12 small fresh or thawed frozen fish balls (½ inch / 12 mm in diameter), or 3 large balls, quartered

1½ cups / 360 ml Sup Kraduuk Muu (Thai pork stock), page 241, hot

5 g / 2 tablespoons pork cracklings, homemade (page 107) or store-bought, very coarsely crumbled

3 g / ½ tablespoon sliced (¼ inch / 6 mm) green onions

1 g / ½ tablespoon coarsely chopped cilantro (thin stems and leaves)

To Serve

Small bowl Sup Kraduuk Muu (Thai pork stock), page 241, including several ribs, hot

Thinly sliced serrano chiles submerged in white vinegar

Thinly sliced fresh Thai chiles submerged in Thai fish sauce

Phrik Pon Khua (Toasted-chile powder), page 233

Granulated sugar

Ground white pepper (from an Asian market)

broth stocked with a few neck bones, which comes from a separate station manned only by a grandma seated beside a big pot. I'd bet the staff goes strong until closing time, just before dawn. ◊ *serves 1*

Note on Serving: You'll notice that this recipe, unlike most Western recipes for noodles, doesn't instruct you to boil a giant bunch of noodles in a pot, then divide them among multiple bowls. This is not spaghetti. In the restaurants that serve Thai noodle soups, each bowl is made to order, assembled one at a time. There is no at-home recipe for noodle soups. When Thai cooks do make noodles at home, they do it the way restaurants do.

Giving a recipe for four bowls would be as strange as telling you to boil and sauce four portions of fettuccine Bolognese separately. That's why I've provided instructions on how to make one bowl. Making more than one is simple. Prepare as many bowls as you want, then one portion at a time, boil the noodles and fish balls in a noodle basket. (If you want to make more bowls more quickly, buy a second noodle basket, though the boiling takes only a minute.) Finish the first bowl, then get to work on the next one.

Prepare the bowl

In a wide soup bowl, combine the lettuce, fish sauce, sugar, and pepper.

Make and serve the soup

Fill a large pot with enough water to submerge the noodle basket. Bring the water to a boil over high heat.

Put the noodles and fish balls in the noodle basket and submerge the basket in the water. Cook, swirling the basket occasionally, until the noodles are just cooked and the fish balls are heated through, about 1 minute.

Firmly shake the basket to drain the ingredients well and dump them into the prepared bowl. Pour the hot stock in the bowl and stir gently. Sprinkle on the cracklings, green onions, and cilantro.

Serve right away with the separate bowl of hot stock with ribs and with serrano and Thai chiles, chile powder, sugar, and pepper to add to taste.

A late-night *muu ping* vendor prepares skewers for passing customers; the sweet grilled pork is also a common breakfast with sticky rice.

MUU PING

หมูปิ้ง   Grilled pork skewers

As a young man and especially now that I'm a certified old dude, I've had plenty of rough mornings in Thailand. You know how it goes. The night before, some old friend shows up with a new bottle just as you're getting ready to call it quits. If I'm in Chiang Mai, the first step to clear my head is a trip to Akha Ama Cafe for a cup of my friend Lee's excellent coffee, made from beans grown in the village outside Chiang Rai, where he grew up. But on the way, I'll stop to grab some breakfast: *khao niaw muu ping*, grilled pork skewers served with sticky rice.

With little more than a table, a charcoal brazier, and a tub of warm sticky rice, *muu ping* peddlers do brisk business late at night or in the early hours. By 7:00 a.m., some vendors already have customers hopping off motor-cycles to grab skewers of the sweet grilled pork. A few hours later, it's all gone and so are they. To habitual cereal eaters or members of the egg-on-toast brigade, this might seem like strange breakfast food, but taken with a generous clump of that sticky rice, fatty pork is just the thing for soaking up booze.

In Thailand, many vendors remove the charred bits from the meat with scissors. At home, it's your call. Either way, keep the heat moderate and your eyes peeled, because the sweet marinade can quickly take the pork across the line from charred to burnt. ◊ *serves 4*

Marinate the pork

Using a sharp knife, cut the pork against the grain into strips about 2 inches / 5 cm long, 1 inch / 2.5 cm wide, and ⅛ inch / 3 mm thick. Do not discard the fat. It's the best part. You should have 36 strips. Put the pork in a bowl and set aside.

Combine the garlic and cilantro root in the mortar and pound to a fine paste, about 30 seconds. Add the sugar and pound to combine. Add the seasoning sauce, fish sauce, oyster sauce, and MSG and stir well. Transfer the mixture to the bowl with the pork and mix with your hands to coat the pork.

Cover and marinate in the fridge for at least 2 hours or up to 4 hours.

Grill the pork

Prepare the grill to cook with medium-high heat (see page 129). Pour the coconut cream into a small bowl.

Thread 3 pork pieces onto each skewer, bunching them together and making sure the tip of the skewer isn't exposed (otherwise it will burn). Put the skewers on a plate or sheet pan and sprinkle them with the pepper. Discard the marinade left in the bowl.

Put the skewers on the grill grate and grill, frequently flipping the skewers and brushing the pork with the coconut cream, until the pork is nicely browned and cooked through, about 10 minutes.

Transfer to a plate and eat right away with the rice.

SPECIAL EQUIPMENT

A Thai granite mortar and pestle

12 wooden skewers, each about 8 inches / 20 cm long, soaked in tepid water for 30 minutes

A grill, preferably charcoal (highly recommended), grate oiled

A food-safe brush

8 ounces / 225 g boneless pork shoulder

3 g / 1 peeled garlic clove

1 g / 1 cilantro root

34 g / 2 tablespoons soft palm sugar

2 teaspoons Thai seasoning sauce (look for the green cap)

1 teaspoon Thai fish sauce

1 teaspoon Thai oyster sauce

2 g / ½ teaspoon MSG (optional but highly recommended)

½ cup / 120 ml well-shaken unsweetened coconut cream, preferably boxed

Ground black pepper

Khao Niaw (Sticky rice), page 248, for serving

KHAI LUAK KAP KHANOM PANG PING

Thai-style coddled eggs with toast ไข่ลวกกับขนมปังปิ้ง

At morning market stalls devoted to *kafae boraan* (coffee brewed old-school, in a sock-shaped strainer) and tea, you'd be wise to order *khai luak* (coddled egg). You'll watch as the vendor drowns an egg in boiling water inside of an empty evaporated milk tin. When the egg is cracked into a cup for serving, it's basically just warmed-up—still more raw than cooked. Along with a few dashes of seasoning sauce and toast, brushed with bright-yellow margarine and cut into "soldiers," it has kick started many days for me in Thailand. ◊ *serves 1*

Put the eggs in a tall, heatproof container with a lid that can hold about 4 cups / 960 ml.

Bring a saucepan of water to a boil. Into the container, pour enough boiling water to cover the eggs by 2 to 3 inches / 5 to 7.5 cm, then cover the container, and let the eggs sit for 4 to 6 minutes, depending on how cooked (from warm to barely set whites) you like your eggs.

Meanwhile, toast the bread, spread on the butter or margarine, and cut each slice into four soldiers. When the eggs are ready, remove them from the water with a slotted spoon and carefully crack the hot eggs directly into a short glass. Season the eggs with the Maggi or soy sauce and pepper. Serve with eggs with the toast soldiers alongside for dipping.

2 eggs, at room temperature

2 slices thick-cut white bread, such as Texas Toast or *shokupan* (Japanese-style white bread)

Butter or margarine to taste

Maggi seasoning sauce or thin soy sauce to taste

Ground white pepper (from an Asian market) to taste

SUNDRY ITEMS

In Thailand, you can drop by the local market to buy cooking staples like freshly made *phrik pon khua* (dried chiles toasted dark in a wok and ground to coarse flakes) or *naam makham piak* (tamarind steeped in hot water and strained to extract a tangy liquid). In the United States, however, most store-bought options are usually best left on the shelf. To make the food in this book, you'll have to prepare some ingredients yourself. Here, you'll find recipes for superior versions of those staples, plus a few other essentials for the dishes in this book.

KHAO KHUA

ข้าวคั่ว Toasted–sticky rice powder

SPECIAL EQUIPMENT
An electric or hand-crank burr grinder

---

200 g / 1 cup uncooked Thai sticky rice (also called glutinous rice or sweet rice)

Raw sticky rice toasted slowly in a wok becomes this pantry staple of Northeastern Thai cooks. Making the ingredient takes patience (low heat and near constant stirring) to ensure the rice grains toast evenly outside and in. In this book, khao khua contributes its toasty quality and subtle crunch to Sup Naw Mai (Isaan bamboo shoot salad), page 166; Tap Waan (Isaan pork liver salad), page 187; and Laap Muu Thawt (Fried minced pork patties), page 79.

◊ *makes about 150 g / 1 cup*

Put the rice in a bowl, add water to cover by 1 inch / 2.5 cm or so, and let the rice soak at room temperature for at least 4 hours or up to overnight. (Alternatively, you can soak the rice in hot tap water for as little as 2 hours.) Drain the rice very well, spread it out in a single layer on kitchen towels, and leave at room temperature until dry to the touch, 30 minutes to 1 hour.

Put the rice in a large, dry frying pan or wok and set over medium-low to low heat (even better, over smoldering charcoal). Cook the rice, stirring almost constantly, until it is evenly light brown (close to the color of peanut butter), 45 minutes to 1 hour. Transfer to a bowl and let cool completely.

Working in batches if necessary, grind the toasted rice to a powder with the texture of coarse sand.

The powder will keep in an airtight container in a cool, dry place for several weeks.

PHRIK PON KHUA

Toasted-chile powder   พริกป่นคั่ว

When moderately spicy dried chiles get slowly toasted until brittle and deep brown, they take on a smoky, tobaccoey flavor that no purchased product can match. Here, Mexican puya chiles stand in for *phrik kaeng*, a dried chile I've seen only in Thailand.

◊ *makes about 22 g / ⅓ cup*

SPECIAL EQUIPMENT
An electric or hand-crank burr grinder

---

1 ounce / 28 g stemmed dried Mexican puya chiles (about 15 chiles)

You might want to open a window and turn on your stove's exhaust fan before you begin.

Put the chiles in a large, dry frying pan or wok on the stove top, turn the heat to high to get the pan hot, and then turn down the heat to medium-low. Cook the chiles, stirring almost constantly and flipping them occasionally so all sides make contact with the hot pan, until very brittle and very dark brown all over, 15 to 20 minutes. Remove the chiles from the pan as they are ready. Discard any seeds that escape from the chiles as they will burn and be bitter.

Let the chiles cool, then working in batches if necessary, grind them to a coarse powder only slightly finer than store-bought red pepper flakes. Immediately transfer to an airtight container.

The powder will keep in an airtight container in a cool, dry place for several weeks.

KRATHIAM JIAW
AND NAAM MAN KRATHIAM

กระเทียมเจียว /
น้ำมันกระเทียม

Fried garlic and garlic oil

SPECIAL EQUIPMENT
A deep-fry thermometer

About 400 g / 2 cups
rendered pork fat,
warmed, or 2 cups /
480 ml neutral oil (such
as soybean or palm)

3 ounces / 85 g peeled
garlic cloves (about
30 cloves), chopped into
about ⅛-inch / 3-mm
pieces

This recipe yields both crunchy, golden bits of garlic and garlic-infused oil, which you can use to fry more garlic or as a remarkably flavorful, aromatic ingredient itself.

◊ *makes about 30 g / 6 tablespoons fried garlic*
  and about 2 cups / 480 ml garlic oil

Set a fine-mesh strainer over a heatproof container. Pour the pork fat or oil to a depth of ¾ inch / 2 cm into a wok or saucepan and heat over high heat to 275°F / 135°C. Use the thermometer to test the temperature, measuring at the center of the vessel and carefully stirring occasionally to ensure a consistent temperature. Line a plate with paper towels and set near the stove.

When hot, add the garlic, then immediately turn down the heat to low and stir well. Cook the garlic, stirring and scraping the sides of the pan occasionally and adjusting the heat to maintain a gentle sizzle, until it is light golden brown and fully crisp, about 10 minutes.

Pour the contents of the pan into the strainer, capturing the oil in the container. Gently shake the strainer to drain the garlic well, then transfer the garlic in more or less a single layer to the prepared plate. Let the garlic and the oil cool completely.

Transfer the fried garlic and the oil to separate airtight containers and store in a cool, dry place. The garlic will keep for up to 2 days and the oil will keep for up to 2 weeks.

HOM JIAW
AND NAAM MAN HOM JIAW

Fried shallots and shallot oil

หอมเจียว /
น้ำมันหอมเจียว

Like the recipe for fried garlic, this one leaves you with both a crunchy fried garnish, sweet with a bitter edge, and flavorful oil.

◊ *makes about 30 g / 6 tablespoons fried shallots and about 2 cups / 480 ml shallot oil*

SPECIAL EQUIPMENT
A deep-fry thermometer

About 400 g / 2 cups rendered pork fat, warmed, or 2 cups / 480 ml neutral oil (such as soybean or palm)

3 ounces / 85 g peeled small shallots, preferably Asian (about 6 shallots), very thinly sliced against the grain

Set a fine-mesh strainer over a heatproof container. Pour the pork fat or oil to a depth of ¾ inch / 2 cm into a wok or saucepan and heat over high heat to 275°F / 135°C. Use the thermometer to test the temperature, measuring at the center of the vessel and carefully stirring occasionally to ensure a consistent temperature. Line a plate with paper towels and set near the stove.

When hot, add the shallots, then immediately turn down the heat to low and stir well. Cook the shallots, stirring and scraping the sides of the pan occasionally and adjusting the heat to maintain a gentle sizzle, until they are deep golden brown and fully crisp, 10 to 20 minutes.

Pour the contents of the pan into the strainer, capturing the oil in the container. Gently shake the strainer to drain the shallots well, then transfer the shallots in more or less a single layer to the prepared plate. Let the shallots and the oil cool completely.

Transfer the fried shallots and the oil to separate airtight containers and store in a cool, dry place. The shallots will keep for up to 2 days and the oil will keep for up to 2 weeks.

NAAM MAKHAM PIAK

น้ำมะขามเปียก   Tamarind water

2 ounces / 55 g Vietnamese or Thai seedless tamarind pulp (also called tamarind paste)

1¾ cups / 420 ml water

Follow this simple process to extract tangy liquid from the sticky, fibrous pulp of the tamarind fruit. Because the result keeps well, the recipe makes more than you'll need for any one recipe. You can even freeze it in ice cube trays, transferring the cubes to freezer bags once they're frozen.

◊ *makes about 1¼ cups / 300 ml*

Combine the pulp and the water in a saucepan and bring to a boil over high heat, breaking up the tamarind as it softens. Immediately turn off the heat, cover the pot, and let the mixture sit until the tamarind is very soft, about 30 minutes.

Set a fine-mesh strainer over a heatproof container. Use a whisk or wooden spoon to mash and stir the tamarind mixture, breaking up any large clumps. Pour the contents of the pan into the strainer, stirring, pressing, and smashing the solids to extract as much liquid as possible. Discard the remaining solids.

The tamarind water will keep in an airtight container in the fridge for up to 1 week and in the freezer for up to 3 months. Stir well before each use.

NAAM CHEUAM
NAAM TAAN PIIP

Palm sugar simple syrup   น้ำเชื่อมน้ำตาลปึ๊บ

To incorporate the complex sweetness of palm sugar into some of the dishes in this book, you must dissolve soft palm sugar in water to make this syrup.

◊ *makes about ½ cup / 120 ml*

2½ ounces / ¼ cup soft palm sugar

¼ cup plus 1 tablespoon / 80 ml water

Combine the sugar and water in a small saucepan, set over medium-low heat, and cook, breaking up the sugar as it softens, just until the sugar has completely dissolved. Remove from the heat and let cool completely.

The syrup will keep in an airtight container in the fridge for up to 2 weeks.

KAPI KUNG

กะปิกุ้ง   Homemade shrimp paste

SPECIAL EQUIPMENT
Cheesecloth
A Thai granite mortar
and pestle

---

500 g / 2 cups jarred
Korean salted shrimp,
preferably Choripdong
brand

35 g / 2 tablespoons Thai
shrimp paste

It takes little effort to make a jury-rigged version of the shrimp paste common to the cooking of my friends in the North of Thailand and all but impossible to find in the States. You essentially combine *kapi* (sometimes spelled *gapi*), the most common Thai fermented shrimp paste and easily found in these parts, with the tiny salted shrimp sold in jars in the refrigerator case of Korean markets. The result is still funky but significantly less intense than regular *kapi*. And without it, dishes like Yam Kop (Northern Thai frog soup), page 49, and Kaeng Awm Neua (Northern Thai stewed beef), page 45, just won't taste right.

◊ *makes about 260 g / 1 cup*

Have ready a double layer of cheesecloth. Briefly rinse and drain the salted shrimp, put them on the cheesecloth, and gently squeeze out most of the liquid. Combine the salted shrimp and shrimp paste in the mortar and pound, stirring occasionally with a spoon, until you have a coarse paste that is more or less an even light brown, 3 to 5 minutes.

The paste will keep in an airtight container in the fridge for up to 6 months.

KUNG HAENG KHUA

Dry-fried dried shrimp กุ้งแห้งคั่ว

Most Asian grocery stores stock different sizes of dried shrimp loose or in bags. Look for medium-size (sometimes you'll just see the letter *M* on the bag) for the recipes in this book. Toasting them brings out their complex flavor and makes them pleasant to chew.

◊ *makes 35 g / ⅓ cup*

45 g / ½ cup medium-size dried shrimp, soaked in water for 10 minutes, then drained

Briefly rinse the drained shrimp and pat them dry. Heat a small dry pan or wok over medium heat, add the shrimp, and cook, stirring frequently, until they are dry all the way through and slightly crispy, 5 to 8 minutes. Set them aside to cool completely.

The dry-fried shrimp will keep in an airtight container at room temperature for up to 1 week.

NAAM BOON SAI

น้ำปูนใส   Limestone water

3 cups / 700 ml water

1 (3½- or 4-ounce / 100- or 115-g) container red or white limestone paste

Slaked lime is a pantry staple in the Thai kitchen. It helps keep fruit firm, even after long cooking. It's an essential part of the concoction of betel nuts and leaves that old-timers chew as a stimulant. And pertinent to the recipes in this book, it helps Thai batters fry exceptionally crisp. The instructions for making *naam boon sai*, a solution of water and slaked lime, barely count as a recipe. Essentially, you mix water and limestone paste (sometimes labeled "lime paste"), which is available in any supermarket with a Southeast Asian section. But a few details deserve note. First, the precise ratio of limestone paste to water isn't important. What's critical is that you use enough paste to hit the saturation point, which is when no more can be dissolved in the water and the remainder settles on the bottom of the container. Second, *naam boon sai* is not this sediment at the bottom but rather the translucent liquid on top. And finally, each time you use *naam boon sai*, refill the jar, shake well, and then let the sediment sink to the bottom. You'll be able to do this a dozen times before you have to buy more paste.

◊ *makes about 3 cups / 700 ml water*

Combine the water and limestone paste in a clear 1-quart / 1-L jar. Stir to dissolve the paste.

Let the mixture sit until the limestone solids settle at the bottom of the jar and the liquid above is no longer cloudy, about 30 minutes. This liquid is *naam boon sai.*

You can use the liquid right away, pouring off the amount needed and making sure the sediment stays behind. You can also cover the jar with an airtight lid and store it at room temperature for as long as there are still flakes on its surface. Be sure to label the container.

After pouring off the liquid, refill the container with water and shake well. Let the solids settle to the bottom, and reserve for the next use.

SUP KRADUUK MUU

Thai pork stock ซุปกระดูกหมู

This is the sort of broth that provides the flavorful base for the famous hangover-halting fish ball noodle soup served at Ong Tipparot in Chiang Mai. But look at the tables next to yours and you'll notice people taking down bowls of the broth itself with a few meaty neck bones plunked in. These bowls make fine partners for the noodles and are also a curative option on their own. This broth is modeled after the one at Ong Tipparot. I essentially simmer a classic Thai pork stock, lightly season it with salt, and don't toss the bones I use to make it, since they're still packed with good stuff to gnaw on. In the States, the pork neck bones you find aren't as meaty as those you see in Thailand, so I use pork ribs instead. These are typically sold precut in Asian markets, but if you buy them elsewhere, ask your butcher to cut them down to a shorter length, about 2 inches (5 centimeters).

◊ *makes about 12 cups / 2.8 L stock and 50 cooked ribs*

Cut the rib racks into individual riblets. Put the ribs in a large pot, fill the pot with cold water, and stir and rub the ribs with your hands. Drain the ribs well. Wipe out the pot, return the ribs to it, and add water to cover the ribs by 1 inch / 2.5 cm or so. Bring the water to a simmer over high heat, then turn off the heat. Skim any scum from the surface, then drain the ribs in a colander and rinse them under running warm water. All of this will rid the ribs of any blood, excess fat bits, and effluvium, which will give you a cleaner-tasting, clearer stock.

Clean the pot, then return the ribs to it and add the water. Bring the water to a rolling simmer over high heat. Cover the pot, turn down the heat to low, maintain a gentle simmer, and cook for 30 minutes.

SPECIAL EQUIPMENT
Cheesecloth
Kitchen twine

2¼ pounds / 1 kg pork baby back ribs, cut crosswise through the bone into racks 2 inches / 5 cm wide

12 cups / 2.8 L water

1 unpeeled garlic head

28 g / 2-inch / 5-cm knob unpeeled fresh ginger

5¼ ounces / 150 g daikon radish (½ medium), cut into rounds about ½ inch / 12 mm thick

3½ ounces / 100 g unpeeled yellow onion (1 small), quartered

4 g / 4 cilantro roots or stems

70 g / 3 green onions, trimmed, very coarsely chopped

30 g / 3 Chinese celery sprigs, very coarsely chopped

9 g / 1 tablespoon white peppercorns (from an Asian market)

9 g / 1 tablespoon kosher salt

◊ ◊ ◊

Meanwhile, using a pestle, a pan, or the flat surface of a knife blade, lightly whack the garlic and ginger to smash them slightly. Put the garlic, ginger, radish, yellow onion, cilantro roots, green onions, celery, and peppercorns on a large piece of cheesecloth, gather the edges around the aromatics, and tie with kitchen twine to secure the bundle. After the ribs have been simmering for 30 minutes, add the bundle and the salt. Re-cover the pot, let the water return to a rolling simmer, and cook until the pork is tender but not falling off the bone, about 30 minutes more.

Discard the cheesecloth bundle. If not using right away, let the stock and meat cool, then transfer to an airtight container and keep in the fridge for up to 4 days.

NAAM JIM SEAFOOD

Spicy, tart dipping sauce for seafood   น้ำจิ้มซีฟู้ด

Charred chiles, lots of garlic, fish sauce, and lime juice charge this dipping sauce with flavor. Fiery and tart, with just enough sugar for balance not sweetness, it provides the spark for Kung Phao (Grilled prawns), page 157. It goes well with most seafood, hence the name it goes by in Thailand, which begins in Thai and ends in English for emphasis.

◊ *makes about 1 cup / 240 ml*

Prepare the grill to cook with medium-high heat (see page 129), or pre-heat a stove-top grill pan over medium-high heat. If using a grill, thread the chiles onto the skewers.

Put the chiles on the grill grate or grill pan and cook, turning them over once or twice, until they are completely blistered and almost completely blackened all over and the flesh is fully soft but not mushy, 5 to 10 minutes; the timing will depend on the size of the chiles. Remove the chiles from the skewers, if used, and use a small knife to peel them as best you can.

Combine the cilantro roots and salt in the mortar and pound to a fairly smooth, slightly fibrous paste, about 30 seconds. Add the garlic and pound until fully incorporated, 1 to 2 minutes. Add the chiles and pound them until you have a fairly smooth paste (the seeds will still be visible), about 1 minute more.

Scrape the paste into a bowl or other container, add the lime juice, fish sauce, and sugar, and stir well. Let the sauce sit for an hour or two before you serve it. Just before serving, stir in the cilantro.

SPECIAL EQUIPMENT

A grill, preferably charcoal (highly recommended), grate oiled (optional)

1 or 2 wooden skewers, soaked in tepid water for 30 minutes, if grilling

A Thai granite mortar and pestle

---

21 g stemmed fresh green Thai (about 14) or serrano (about 3) chiles

7 g / 7 cilantro roots

1 g / ½ teaspoon kosher salt

21 g / 7 peeled garlic cloves, halved lengthwise

6 tablespoons / 90 ml fresh lime juice, preferably from Key limes or from regular (Persian) limes spiked with a small squeeze of Meyer lemon juice

¼ cup / 60 ml Thai fish sauce

20 g / 1 tablespoon plus 2 teaspoons granulated sugar

4 g / 2 tablespoons coarsely chopped cilantro (thin stems and leaves)

NAAM JIM KAI

น้ำจิ้มไก่   Sweet chile dipping sauce

SPECIAL EQUIPMENT
A Thai granite mortar
and pestle

---

200 g / 1 cup granulated
sugar

¼ cup plus 2 tablespoons /
90 ml distilled white
vinegar, preferably a Thai
brand

½ cup / 120 ml water

21 g stemmed fresh or
drained pickled red Thai
chiles, coarsely sliced

1¼ ounces / 35 g peeled
garlic cloves, halved
lengthwise

3 g / 1 teaspoon kosher
salt

This is a far superior version of the familiar tooth-achingly sugary sauce on the shelf at supermarkets. The real thing, too, is plenty sweet, but here the sweetness is tempered by the acidity of vinegar and the heat of Thai chiles. In this book, this sauce is meant for Plaa Meuk Ping (Grilled dried cuttlefish), page 32, and En Kai Thawt (Fried chicken tendons), page 88, and is used as part of the dressing for Som Tam Thawt (Fried papaya salad), page 101.

◊ *makes about 1¼ cups / 300 ml*

Combine the sugar, vinegar, and water in a saucepan, set over high heat, and bring to a vigorous simmer, whisking to dissolve the sugar. Cook for 5 minutes or so, continuing to whisk as needed.

Meanwhile, combine the chiles, garlic, and salt in the mortar and pound to a very coarse paste. Add the chile mixture to the saucepan, lower the heat to maintain a steady simmer, and cook until the liquid thickens a bit and becomes slightly syrupy, 8 to 12 minutes. Remove from the heat and let cool to room temperature.

The sauce can be used right away, or it will keep in an airtight container in the fridge for up to a few months.

JAEW

Isaan dipping sauce   แจ่ว

While Naam Jim Seafood (Spicy, tart dipping sauce for seafood), page 243, is fueled by bright acidity and the fire and fragrance of fresh chiles, this dipping sauce has a darker flavor. Soy sauce teams up with fish sauce to deliver umami. Tobaccoey dried chiles provide heat and, along with lemongrass and a last-minute dose of toasted-rice powder, aroma. The sauce enhances most grilled meat, including Muu Yaang Thawt (Fried grilled pork), page 115, and Tap Kai / Tap Pet Ping (Grilled chicken / duck liver skewers), page 153.

◊ *makes about ½ cup / 120 ml*

Pound the lemongrass in the mortar until you have a coarse, fibrous paste, about 30 seconds. Scrape the paste into a bowl and stir in the fish sauce, soy sauce, seasoning sauce, lime juice, simple syrup, and chile powder. Let sit at room temperature for at least 1 hour (it'll get even better) or in the fridge for up to 2 days (bring to room temperature before serving).

Just before serving, stir in the rice powder and cilantro.

SPECIAL EQUIPMENT
A Thai granite mortar and pestle

Sauce

10 g / 1 heaping tablespoon thinly sliced lemongrass (tender parts only), about 2 large stalks

2 tablespoons Thai fish sauce

1½ tablespoons Thai thin soy sauce

¾ teaspoon Thai seasoning sauce (look for the green cap)

3½ tablespoons / 105 ml fresh lime juice, preferably from Key limes or from regular (Persian) limes spiked with a small squeeze of Meyer lemon juice

1½ tablespoons Naam Cheuam Naam Taan Piip (Palm sugar simple syrup), page 237

5 g / 1½ tablespoons Phrik Pon Khua (Toasted-chile powder), page 233

To Finish

9 g / 1 tablespoon Khao Khua (Toasted–sticky rice powder), page 232

2 g / 1 tablespoon coarsely chopped cilantro (thin stems and leaves)

MUU DENG

หมูเด้ง   Bouncy pork balls

SPECIAL EQUIPMENT
A Thai granite mortar
and pestle

---

15 g / 5 peeled garlic
cloves, halved lengthwise

3 g / 3 cilantro roots

Less than 1 g / ¼ teaspoon
black peppercorns

1 g / ½ teaspoon
kosher salt

1 egg white, at room
temperature

8 ounces / 225 g ground
pork (not lean)

2 teaspoons Thai fish sauce

The key to these meatballs is doing what so many recipes tell you not to. Here, you *want* to overmix. Briefly boiled, the result has a dense, squeaky texture and a flavor so enjoyable that it'll supposedly make you bounce out of your seat—hence the nickname of these orbs. They make a fine addition to Jok (Rice porridge), page 217, and Khao Tom (Rice soup), page 214.

◊ *makes about 35 balls*

Bring a large pot of water to a simmer.

Meanwhile, combine the garlic, cilantro roots, peppercorns, and salt in the mortar and pound to a fairly smooth, slightly fibrous paste, about 1 minute.

Vigorously beat the egg white in a bowl until white, frothy, and nearly doubled in volume, about 45 seconds. Add the pork, paste, and fish sauce to the egg white and use your hand to stir and squish the mixture until all of the ingredients are well combined. Next, spend 2 minutes or so alternating between firmly mixing for about 10 seconds and picking up the mixture, steadying the bowl with your free hand, and forcefully throwing the mixture into the bowl.

Transfer the mixture to a resealable plastic bag and work it toward a corner, twisting the bag to force the mixture into the corner and firmly shaking to eliminate any air pockets. Use scissors to snip a 1- to 1½-inch (2.5- to 4-cm) wide opening from the corner.

Hold the bag a couple of inches above the simmering water with one hand and hold the scissors or a small knife with the other. Squeeze the bag slightly to force out about 1 inch / 2.5 cm of the mixture and use the scissors or knife to coax the rough sphere into the water. Repeat until one-third of the mixture is in the water. Cook until the balls float to the surface and are just cooked through, 1 to 2 minutes. Use a slotted spoon to scoop the balls into a bowl as they are ready. Repeat with the remaining meat mixture in two batches.

The balls can be used right away, or they will keep in an airtight container in the fridge for up to 5 days or in resealable plastic bags in the freezer for up to 6 months.

KHAO HOM MALI

Jasmine rice ข้าวหอมมะลิ

While this book is specifically about food that isn't necessarily served with rice, I'd be remiss if I withheld a recipe for jasmine rice—the rice of choice in Central and Southern Thailand as well as in a small pocket of Northern Thailand near Mae Hong Son. Truth be told, the aromatic, pleasantly bland grains go well with the stir-fried dishes (page 199) in this book. Do yourself a favor, though. Buy jasmine rice grown in Thailand, which tends to have plenty of *hom* (aroma), rinse it as instructed (to wash away some of the starch and avoid clumpy, mushy rice), and cook it, as the vast majority of Thai cooks do, in a simple electric rice cooker rather than in a pot.

◊ *makes about 900 g / 6 cups*

SPECIAL EQUIPMENT
An electric rice cooker

———

400 g / 2 cups uncooked Thai jasmine rice

2 cups / 480 ml water

Put the rice in a fine-mesh strainer set inside a large bowl. Fill the bowl with enough cool tap water to cover the rice by an inch or so (2.5 to 5 cm) and use your hand to stir the rice gently. Lift the strainer, dump out the cloudy water, and repeat the process until the water is no longer cloudy, about three times. Drain the rice, gently shaking it occasionally, until it's fully dry to the touch, about 15 minutes.

Put the rice in a rice cooker in an even layer. Add the water, cover with the lid, press the button, and let the cooker do its thing. Once it's done, let the rice sit in the rice cooker with the cover on for about 20 minutes. Don't skip this step. It allows some of the steam to dissipate and some to get reabsorbed into the rice. It keeps the rice from clumping and gives the grains a chance to cool slightly, so when you fluff the rice, the grains aren't so soft that they break.

Finally, fluff the rice: use a spoon to gently rake the top few layers of rice to separate the grains, and gradually rake the next few layers and so on, working your way toward the bottom. Try your best not to break or smash the grains. The rice keeps for several hours after fluffing in the rice cooker on its "Warm" setting.

Cooled, leftover jasmine rice keeps in a covered container in the fridge. Day-old rice is perfect for Khao Tom (Rice soup), page 214.

KHAO NIAW

ข้าวเหนียว Sticky rice

SPECIAL EQUIPMENT
A sticky rice steamer set
(woven basket and pot)
Cheesecloth

795 g / 4 cups uncooked
Thai sticky rice (also called
glutinous rice or sweet rice)

In my first book, recipes for rice come before all of the others. That's because even though curries and fiery "salads" get the glory, rice—whether glutinous grains in the North and Northeast or jasmine rice elsewhere—is the essence of the Thai meal, the crux of the cuisine. But in this book, rice is consigned to the very end, because unlike so many dishes in the first book, the dishes in this one aren't meant to make up a proper meal. Instead, they are designed to entertain you as you consume booze. So although rice would be a welcome addition to most of what you cook from this book, it's optional. And here you'll only find a recipe for the sticky variety common in the North of Thailand, where I've spent the vast majority of my time in the country and where it's common practice to grab little clumps from a mass of chewy glutinous grains to use as a sort of edible eating implement. Those who haven't made sticky rice will be surprised at how simple the process is: you just soak, rinse, then steam the grains. Unlike most rice, which is referred to as steamed even though it's actually boiled, sticky rice is in fact set over bubbling water and cooked with the moist heat of the vapor. Cooks have come up with many ways to avoid using the customary woven basket and potbellied pot (see page 257), but do yourself a favor and spend the twenty bucks.

◊ *makes about 1.2 kg / 6½ cups*

Put the sticky rice in a large bowl, add tepid tap water to cover by 1 to 2 inches / 2.5 to 5 cm, and let soak for at least 4 hours or up to 10 hours. Alternatively, you can soak the rice in hot tap water for 2 hours.

Drain the rice in a fine-mesh strainer held over the sink, then set the strainer with the rice inside a large bowl. Fill the bowl with enough cool tap water to cover the rice by an inch or so (2.5 to 5 cm) and use your hand to stir the rice gently. Lift the strainer, dump out the cloudy water, and repeat the process until the water is no longer cloudy, about three times.

Pour water to a depth of about 2 inches / 5 cm into the sticky rice steamer pot and bring to a boil over high heat. Line the steamer basket with a double layer of damp cheesecloth, and transfer the rice to the basket. Fold the cheesecloth so it covers the rice, pat the bundle to flatten the top and cover with a pot lid or with a clean, damp kitchen cloth, tucking it around the bundle.

Lower the heat so the water in the steamer pot is at a steady but not furious boil and set the basket in the pot. Cook, carefully flipping the bundle after 15 minutes, until the grains in the center are fully tender but still chewy (almost springy) and not mushy, 30 to 35 minutes.

Transfer the rice to an insulated container, like a cooler, or to a large bowl covered with a plate. Wait for about 15 minutes before digging in. The sticky rice will stay warm for 30 minutes or so.

INGREDIENTS

Once you collect half a dozen bottled sauces and a handful of fresh ingredients—many of which, like Thai chiles, galangal, and makrut lime leaves, to name a few, keep well in the freezer—the food in this book becomes a lot easier to cook. Here is a rundown of some of the most commonly used ingredients that require explanation.

Unless otherwise noted, you'll find these items at Asian markets that specialize in Southeast Asian foods or have a robust Southeast Asian section. Plus, nowadays, even many supermarkets stock Thai chiles, lemongrass, and turmeric root. A few ingredients, however, require a bit of searching. To locate the Thai herb *phak chii farang*, you might find yourself at a Vietnamese market (where it goes by *ngò gai*) or a Latin one (where it is called *recao* or *culantro*). Mexican markets stock dried puya chiles, which I've found to be the best stand-in for the hard-to-find Thai chile *phrik kaeng*. Your local farmers' market might sell Thai basil, cilantro with the roots on, and goat horn chiles. If you're stymied, there's always the megastore known as the Internet.

◊ ◊ ◊

Banana leaf (*bai yok*)

Primarily used to wrap fish and meat before grilling, banana leaves impart a subtle tannic flavor and aroma. They're occasionally available fresh but are more typically sold frozen in Asian and Latin markets (where they go by *hoja de platano*).

Blood (*leuat*)

Used to enrich the flavor of dishes like boat noodles and Northern Thai *laap*, raw blood can be found in the freezer case at Korean and Chinese markets or at butcher shops that work closely with small local farms and allow special orders.

Chinese celery (*kheun chai*)

A common ingredient in stir-fries and soups, this variety is leafier and has much thinner stems than the celery ubiquitous in supermarkets in the States. Look for it in the produce section of Asian markets.

Chinese keys (*krachai*)

You'll likely only find this rhizome frozen in the United States, which works well for the recipes in this book. Look for it, whole or shredded, in Chinese and Southeast Asian markets, where it might also be labeled *grachai* or *krachai*. It's sometimes referred to as lesser galangal, Chinese keys, or simply rhizome. Avoid canned or jarred *krachai*.

Cilantro root (*rak phak chii*)

In the United States, cilantro (or coriander) is typically sold without its root attached. When you see roots-on bunches at farmers' markets and Southeast Asian grocery stores, buy them (or ask if you can place a special order). Thinly slice the roots you don't use after several days and freeze them. The root adds the punchy flavor without the *men khiaw* (the strong green quality that some call "soapiness") of the leaves.

Coriander seeds (*met phak chii*)

Those eager to go the extra mile will use the coriander seeds sold at Asian grocery stores rather than the ones available at your local supermarket. The Asian seeds have a nutty, spicy quality, while the Western ones call to mind hot dogs a bit too vividly for my taste.

Dried long peppers (*dippli*)

Most good spice shops carry this variety of dried pepper, which is occasionally used in Northern Thai cooking and has a complex, less harsh flavor than common black peppercorns. Called *pippali* in Indian and Malay it's most readily available at specialty spice shops and online.

Fish sauce (*naam plaa*)

Look for bottles of this intensely salty seasoning and condiment made from salted, fermented fish on shelves in Asian markets. For Thai fish sauce, the Squid and Tiparos brands are solid (avoid the common Thai Kitchen brand) and Megachef is best. Avoid

Vietnamese brands for the recipes in this book. They are mild and sweet in comparison to Thai brands, a different flavor profile for a different cuisine.

Galangal (*khaa*)

Pounded into many seasoning pastes, this knobby rhizome looks like pale-skinned ginger but tastes citrusy, almost soapy, and much less sharp than its kin. Find it fresh in Thai and some Chinese grocery stores in the refrigerated section or near the produce and in the freezer section of many Asian markets.

Gouramy fish, pickled (*plaa raa*)

This fermented fish (also called *pa laa, ba laa*, or other similar phonetic transliteration; *mắm cá sặc* in Vietnamese; and "salted gourami"), sold in jars, is a common ingredient in the cooking of North and Northeastern Thailand. Look for Pantainorasingh brand or other brands that sell whole fish or fillets (not "creamy" or "cream style") in the same aisle where you spot jarred sauces and condiments.

Green Anaheim, Hungarian wax, and goat horn chiles

Look for these fresh chiles—which mimic the relatively mild heat, flavor, and aroma of certain Thai chiles used in stir-fries and chile dips—at supermarkets and at farmers' markets in the summer. The long (about 6 inches / 15 cm) unnamed green chiles sold in Asian markets in the States will also do the trick.

Holy basil (bai kaphrao)

Holy basil, also known as hot basil, which has a peppery flavor and intense, distinctive aroma, is used most famously in a Thai stir-fry of ground pork or chicken. Your best bet for finding it is a Thai-focused market (ask for by ga-POW). Beware, however, as I've seen the label holy basil attached to purple-stemmed Thai or sweet basil.

Lemongrass (takhrai)

Lemongrass has become fairly common in big-city markets, Asian and not. Many recipes call for the soft, tender heart of the stalk. The size and freshness will affect the yield of thinly sliced tender parts, though you can figure on about 7 g / 1 tablespoon for every large stalk. To access it, remove 1 inch / 2.5 cm from the bottom and about 9 inches / 23 cm from the top of the stalk. Next, peel off the fibrous layers. After 5 layers, you should have reached the tender portion. Start slicing at the bottom, discarding any parts that give a sharp knife pause.

Makhwen

The dried seeds of the Northern Thai prickly ash tree (*Zanthoxylum limonella* Alston), used as a spice in some Northern Thai dishes, are hard but not impossible to find in the West. Ask around at Thai markets and poke around online. Look for creative descriptions like "Thai Sichuan peppercorns."

Makrut lime leaves (bai makrut)

The fragrant leaves of the makrut lime tree are available fresh (typically in the refrigerated section) or frozen in Thai and some Asian or Indian grocery stores. Do not use dried leaves. If you don't use fresh leaves within a couple of days of purchasing them, freeze them for up to 3 months.

MSG (phong chu roht)

A few recipes in this book call for this maligned ingredient, so grab a bag of monosodium glutamate. The white stuff is often sold under the Japanese Ajinomoto brand, but sometimes, especially in Western stores, it is labeled Accent.

Oyster sauce (naam man hoi)

A common bottled seasoning in Thai cooking, oyster sauce should have a salty, briny flavor along with a mellow sweetness, not just an intense saltiness. To achieve the right flavor for the recipes in this book, buy a Thai brand, such as Maekrua, which you'll find at Southeast Asian and most Chinese markets.

Palm sugar (naam taan)

Soft palm sugar (*naam taan piip*) is sold in small plastic containers at Thai markets. A gentle squeeze will tell you if it's hardened from improper storage. If you must, you can buy palm sugar in hard disk form (*naam taan beuk*) and approximate the soft stuff by microwaving it with a splash of water just until it softens. Either way, look for brands that sell 100 percent palm sugar from Thailand, such as Golden Chef or Cock.

Puya chiles, dried

This Mexican chile (sometimes spelled *pulla*) mimics the size and flavor of *phrik kaeng*, a medium-size dried chile used in Thailand. Puya chiles are available in Mexican and Latin markets, the "Latin foods" section of some supermarkets, and online. If the chiles are particularly supple, leaving them uncovered for a day will make them brittle and easier for novices to pound as instructed in the recipes.

Salted radish (hua chai po)

You'll find this pale ruddy brown product, also labeled preserved radish, on shelves at Asian markets. Look for a Thai brand sold in a bag, either shredded or whole (not minced). My recipes call for the preshredded version; if you can only find whole, cut them crosswise into 1/8-inch-thick slices, then lay those flat and cut them into very thin strips.

Sawtooth herb (phak chii farang)

This long, serrated leaf (also called saw-leaf herb) is added to Northern Thai soups, curries, and salads. A better bet than Thai markets, which tend not to stock specifically Northern Thai products, are Latin ones, where the herb goes by *culantro* and *recao*, and Vietnamese ones, where it goes by *ngò gai*.

Seasoning sauce (*sauce phrung roht*)

Yes, it's labeled seasoning sauce. In Thai, it's *sauce phrung roht* (sauce to adjust flavor). Made from fermented soybeans, salt, sugar, and other ingredients, it provides Worcestershire sauce–like flavor enhancement but without the dried-spice component. Look for Thai brand bottles, such as Golden Mountain and Healthy Boy, which almost always have a green cap.

Shallots, Asian (*hom daeng*)

For shallots that are to be pounded into pastes for stir-fries, soups, stews, and so on, my preference is for the small, round shallots sold at Chinese and Southeast Asian markets, which have a more appropriate size and flavor and lower water content than torpedo-shaped French shallots.

Shaoxing wine (*lao jiin*)

This Chinese wine made from brown glutinous rice is occasionally used in Thai dishes, including a couple in this book. Buy it at Asian markets, where you might see the name spelled on labels in several phonetic transliterations, and opt for bottles that don't say cooking wine.

Soy sauce, black (*si ew dam*)

One of three types of soy sauce common in Thai cooking, black soy has a strong, molasses-like character and tastes markedly more sweet than thin soy sauce. Seek out Thai brands, such as Kwong Hung Seng (look for the dragonfly on the label), Healthy Boy, or Maekrua at Chinese and Southeast Asian markets.

Soy sauce, sweet (*si ew waan*)

Sweet soy is very sweet compared to the molasses-like sweetness of black soy. Seek out Thai brands, such as Kwong Hung Seng (look for the dragonfly on the label), Healthy Boy, or Maekrua at Chinese and Southeast Asian markets.

Soy sauce, thin (*si ew khao*)

Thin soy is salty without a particularly intense flavor. Seek out Thai brands, such as Kwong Hung Seng (look for the dragonfly on the label), Healthy Boy, or Maekrua at Chinese and Southeast Asian markets.

Tamarind (*makham piak*)

Sometimes called paste or even just tamarind, the tart seedless pulp is sold in bagged blocks at Chinese and Southeast Asian markets and in some supermarkets and Latin grocery stores. Buy Vietnamese or Thai brands, such as Cock. Tamarind is a common seasoning in Thailand, especially in the North.

Thai basil (*bai horapha*)

This licorice-scented variety, sometimes called sweet basil, makes an aromatic addition to soups and stir-fries. Look for it at Chinese and Southeast Asian markets and at farmers' markets. Thai basil has distinctive purple stems, which makes it easy to identify, even if the herb is labeled simply basil.

Thai chiles, dried (*phrik haeng*)

Pounded into pastes or added whole to stir-fries and salads, these chiles, which are 2 to 3 inches / 5 to 7.5 cm long, are available online as well as in Southeast Asian–focused grocery stores. Look for bags that specify "from Thailand." If all else fails, the dried chiles available in most Asian markets will do.

Thai chiles, fresh (*phrik khii nuu*)

You will find these small (2 inches / 5 cm long), fiery chiles at Asian and particularly Southeast Asian markets and some big-city markets, where they might be labeled bird, bird's eye, or occasionally finger chile. Frozen ones are fine (they actually tend to have a more consistent heat level).

White pepper (*phrik thai khao*)

To my taste, the white pepper sold under Asian, and especially Thai brands, has a much milder, more pleasant flavor than the stuff on offer at Western markets.

Yellow turmeric root (*khamin*)

Yellow turmeric is stocked fresh in Indian, West Indian, and some Thai grocery stores (and even certain high-end supermarkets) and in the freezer section of many Asian stores. Unlike its white cousin, it's not slivered and eaten raw but rather pounded into pastes for curries, soups, and the like, particularly in the North.

EQUIPMENT

If you're going to make recipes from this book, you'll want to invest in some equipment. While using some of this cookware is merely extremely helpful, much of it is vital to the food. Without a granite mortar and proper wok, for instance, you might as well just order takeout.

Charcoal grill

The recipes in this book that require grilling can be executed on a gas grill. Yet without the flavor and aroma bestowed by smoldering charcoal, the finished food will be missing an important element. The committed among you will be sure to use a charcoal grill, especially one that allows you to adjust the height of the grate. For more on Thai grilling, see page 129.

Chopping block

To chop pork properly for Laap Neua Dip (Nan-style minced raw beef "salad"), page 188, and to whack beef safely for Jin Tup (Hammered flank steak), page 135, buy a solid wooden chopping block. Look for one that is about 2 inches / 5 cm thick.

Granite mortar and pestle

This sturdy, squat stone mortar and matching pestle is essential for pounding pastes. This pair is available at Thai and many Asian markets, good cookware stores (Asian and not), and online. Look for a mortar with an opening at least 6 inches / 15 cm in diameter.

Long-handled noodle basket

Available at Asian markets, cookware shops, and online, this is essentially a mesh strainer with a deep basket meant for holding noodles submerged in boiling water. Buy two, which will make many noodle dishes twice as quick to cook.

Scale

To guide you adequately to the flavors you're after, the recipes in this book demand measurements that are more precise than usual. Don't be put off by all of the grams and ounces. Buy a cheap digital food scale that can be switched between US and metric measuring modes. It'll help you cook from this book and many others.

Spider skimmer

To scoop food efficiently from bubbling oil or water, you can't do better than the shallow mesh basket of a spider skimmer. Any good store that sells cookware should stock them, but your best bet for a good price is a shop that specializes in Asian equipment.

Sticky rice steamer set

To make sticky rice properly, you need this inexpensive set: a woven basket that is set atop an aluminum potbellied pot. Shop for it in markets with a Southeast Asian section and online.

Wok

The best option for an American stove is an 11- to 14-inch / 28- to 35-cm flat-bottomed wok pan made of aluminum, stainless steel, or carbon steel. (If you have an electric stove, consider cast iron.) At the moment, my preferred brand for home use is Vollrath. One exception: For Naam Phrik Khaa (Galangal chile dip), page 67, I recommend a nonstick wok.

Wok spatula

Stir-frying (constantly stirring, scooping, and flipping ingredients in a hot wok) is made infinitely easier with this spatula, which looks like a little shovel. Buy a wooden one if you have a nonstick wok; otherwise, a sturdy metal one is great.

ACKNOWLEDGMENTS

This book is dedicated to the people of Thailand to whom I owe so much. Your generous spirit and the sense of fun with which you approach all endeavors (including having a few drinks), is an inspiration.

Thank you to all the *khii mao*, food vendors, restaurateurs, cooks, distillers, farmers, market stall owners, friends, comrades and family in Thailand, thank you so much for your tutelage and for sharing your knowledge. I am forever your humble student.

Dear Kung, thanks for putting up with me, supporting me, schooling me and being the best mom and personal photographer that three absurd cats could hope for.

Thank you, Tony Bourdain, for making an episode of *Parts Unknown* based on drinking and eating in Northern Thailand, thereby bringing a better understanding of the food, booze and culture to a wider audience than I ever could on my own. I am honored to have shared adventure, conversation and hoisted a few with you; hopefully that *luu* won't come back to haunt you.

Thanks to Austin Bush and Adam Levey, our intrepid photo team, for another realization of an unconventional concept and for your flexibility in pursuit of getting it right. Also, thanks Austin for being a generous sharer of knowledge and interpreter on our travels.

David Thompson, thanks for your counsel and showing me how a chef is supposed to comport himself, both in the kitchen and out … I'll let that hang out in the breeze, with love.

Kimberly Witherspoon, my agent extraordinaire and always the smartest person in the room; knowing that you've got my back gives me a lot of serenity.

Khun Nick Bhirombhakdi, chef Ian Kittichai and chef McDang, thanks for humoring me, telling good and valuable stories; much respect.

JJ Goode, my long-suffering co-writer and buddy, thanks for not murdering me during the more stressful times of pasting this bastard together.

Shout out to Jessica Wang and Kat Craddock for recipe testing under tight deadlines.

Lee Ayu Chuepa and the whole Akha Ama crew, who fueled a lot of this enterprise with killer coffee; thanks for the inspiration!

To the Pok Pok Restaurants team, thanks for holding down the fort while I was gadding about Thailand in pursuit of this project.

Thank you to the intrepid Ten Speed crew: Aaron Wehner, Jenny Wapner, Emily Timberlake, Kara Plikaitis. Well, that's a wrap. Now let's make another one!

Khop khun maak khrap, thuk khon!

INDEX

A

Aep Samoeng Muu (Pig's brains grilled in banana leaf), 141–43

Anchovies
dried, 23
Plaa Lek Thawt Krob (Fried tiny fish), 23–25

B

Bamboo shoots
Sup Naw Mai (Isaan bamboo shoot salad), 166–69
Banana leaves, 252
Basil
holy, 253
Thai, 254
BBQ (Thai-style barbecue beef skewers), 137–38
Beef
BBQ (Thai-style barbecue beef skewers), 137–38
Jin Tup (Hammered flank steak), 135–36
Kaeng Awm (Northern Thai stewed beef), 45–47
Laap Neua Dip (Nan-style minced raw beef "salad"), 188–91
Mam (Isaan beef and liver sausage), 117–21
Neua Daet Diaw (Fried semidried beef), 91–92
Phat Khii Mao (Drunkard's stir-fry), 201–4
Beer, 73–74
Blood, 252
Tom Leuat Muu (Pork soup with steamed blood cakes and offal), 219–21
Bread
Khai Luak Kap Khanom Pang Ping (Thai-style coddled eggs with toast), 229

C

Cashews
Yam Met Mamuang Himaphaan (Fried cashews with salt, chiles, and green onions), 37–38
Chicken
En Kai Thawt (Fried chicken tendons), 88–90
Kai Thawt (Thai-style fried chicken), 95–97
Khua Haem Pik Kai (Stir-fried chicken wings with hot basil and chiles), 205–8
Tap Kai Ping (Grilled chicken liver skewers), 153–55
Tom Som Kai Baan (Sour Northern Thai "village chicken" soup), 57–59
Chiles
Naam Jim Kai (Sweet chile dipping sauce), 244
Naam Phrik Khaa (Galangal chile dip), 67–68
Naam Phrik Num (Green chile dip), 71–72
Naam Phrik Taa Daeng (Red-eye chile dip), 63–66
Phrik Kleua (Salt-chile dip for green mango), 35
Phrik Pon Khua (Toasted-chile powder), 233
varieties of, 252, 253, 254
Chinese celery, 252
Chinese keys, 252
Chopping blocks, 257
Cilantro root, 252
Clams
Phat Hoi Laai Samun Phrai (Stir-fried clams with krachai, galangal, and Thai basil), 209–11
Coriander seeds, 252
Cuttlefish
Plaa Meuk Ping (Grilled dried cuttlefish), 32–33

D

Dipping sauces
    Jaew (Isaan dipping sauce), 245
    Naam Jim Kai (Sweet chile
        dipping sauce), 244
    Naam Jim Seafood (Spicy, tart
        dipping sauce for seafood),
        243
    Naam Phrik Khaa (Galangal
        chile dip), 67–68
Drinks
    beer, 73–74
    Lao Khao (Rice whiskey), 11–17
    whiskey soda, 162
    Ya Dawng (Herbal rice
        whiskey), 40
Duck
    Tap Pet Ping (Grilled duck liver
        skewers), 153–55

E

Eggs
    Jin Som Mok Khai (Sour pork
        and egg grilled in banana
        leaves), 158–60
    Jok (Rice porridge), 217–18
    Khai Luak Kap Khanom Pang
        Ping (Thai-style coddled eggs
        with toast), 229
    Khao Tom (Rice soup), 214–15
    soft-poached, 218
En Kai Thawt (Fried chicken
    tendons), 88–90
Equipment, 9, 257

F

Fish
    gouramy, pickled, 252
    Kuaytiaw Luuk Chin Plaa Hua
        Nom (Noodle soup with tiny
        fish balls), 223–24
    Plaa Lek Thawt Krob (Fried tiny
        fish), 23–25
    Yam Plaa Salit (Fried gouramy
        fish salad), 174–76
Fish sauce, 252

F

Frog
    Yam Kop (Northern Thai frog
        soup), 49–51

G

Galangal, 252
    Naam Phrik Khaa (Galangal
        chile dip), 67–68
Garlic
    Krathiam Jiaw (Fried garlic), 234
    Naam Man Krathiam (Garlic
        oil), 234
Grilling
    equipment, 257
    tips, 129–31

H

Hang Muu Yaang (Grilled pig's
    tails), 144–46
Holy basil, 253
Hom Jiaw (Fried shallots), 235
Huu Muu Thawt (Fried pig's ears),
    84–85

J

Jaew (Isaan dipping sauce), 245
Jin Som Mok Khai (Sour pork and
    egg grilled in banana leaves),
    158–60
Jin Tup (Hammered flank steak),
    135–36
Jok (Rice porridge), 217–18

K

Kaeng Awm (Northern Thai
    stewed beef), 45–47
Kai Saam Yang (Chicken three
    ways), 20–22
Kai Thawt (Thai-style fried
    chicken), 95–97
Kapi Kung (Homemade shrimp
    paste), 238
Khaep Muu (Pork cracklings),
    107–8
Khai Luak Kap Khanom Pang Ping
    (Thai-style coddled eggs with
    toast), 229

Khao Hom Mali (Jasmine rice), 247

Khao Khua (Toasted-sticky rice powder), 232

Khao Niaw (Sticky rice), 248–49

Khao Tom (Rice soup), 214–15

Kheun chai, 252

Khua Haem Pik Kai (Stir-fried chicken wings with hot basil and chiles), 205–8

Krachai, 252

Krathiam Jiaw (Fried garlic), 234

Kuaytiaw Luuk Chin Plaa Hua Nom (Noodle soup with tiny fish balls), 223–24

Kung Haeng Khua (Dry-fried dried shrimp), 239

Kung Phao (Grilled prawns), 157

Kung Ten (Dancing shrimp), 29–30

L

Laap Neua Dip (Nan-style minced raw beef "salad"), 188–91

Laap Muu Thawt (Fried minced pork patties), 79–81

Laap Phrae (Phrae-style minced pork "salad"), 192–97

Lao Khao (Rice whiskey), 11–17

Lemongrass, 253

Limes
    Jaew (Isaan dipping sauce), 245
    Kai Saam Yang (Chicken three ways), 20–22
    Naam Jim Seafood (Spicy, tart dipping sauce for seafood), 243

Limestone paste
    Naam Boon Sai (Limestone water), 240

Long beans
    Phat Khii Mao (Drunkard's stir-fry), 201–4
    Som Tam Thawt (Fried papaya salad), 101–3

Long peppers, dried, 252

M

Makhwen, 253

Makrut lime leaves, 253

Mam (Isaan beef and liver sausage), 117–21

Mangoes
    Phrik Kleua (Salt-chile dip for green mango), 35

Mortar and pestle, 9, 257

Mouse ear mushroom. See White fungus

MSG, 253

Muu Daet Diaw (Fried semidried pork), 91–92

Muu Deng (Bouncy pork balls), 246

Muu Ping (Grilled pork skewers), 226–27

Muu Yaang Thawt (Fried grilled pork), 115–16

N

Naam Boon Sai (Limestone water), 240

Naam Cheuam Naam Taan Piip (Palm sugar simple syrup), 237

Naam Jim Kai (Sweet chile dipping sauce), 244

Naam Jim Seafood (Spicy, tart dipping sauce for seafood), 243

Naam Makham Piak (Tamarind water), 236

Naam Man Hom Jiaw (Shallot oil), 235

Naam Man Krathiam (Garlic oil), 234

Naam Phrik Khaa (Galangal chile dip), 67–68

Naam Phrik Num (Green chile dip), 71–72

Naam Phrik Taa Daeng (Red-eye chile dip), 63–66

Naem Sii Khrong Muu (Fried sour pork ribs), 109–13

Neua Daet Diaw (Fried semidried beef), 91–92

Noodle baskets, 257

Noodles
    glass, 177
    Jok (Rice porridge), 217–18
    Kuaytiaw Luuk Chin Plaa Hua Nom (Noodle soup with tiny fish balls), 223–24
    Yam Mama (Instant-noodle salad), 180–81
    Yam Wun Sen (Glass noodle salad), 177–79

O

Oils
Naam Man Hom Jiaw (Shallot oil), 235
Naam Man Krathiam (Garlic oil), 234
Oyster sauce, 253

P

Palm sugar, 253
Naam Cheuam Naam Taan Piip (Palm sugar simple syrup), 237
Papayas
Som Tam Thawt (Fried papaya salad), 101–3
Peanuts
Kai Saam Yang (Chicken three ways), 20–22
Som Tam Thawt (Fried papaya salad), 101–3
Thua Thawt Samun Phrai (Fried peanuts with makrut lime leaves, garlic, and chiles), 26–28
Phat Hoi Laai Samun Phrai (Stir-fried clams with krachai, galangal, and Thai basil), 209–11
Phat Khii Mao (Drunkard's stir-fry), 201–4
Phrik Kleua (Salt-chile dip for green mango), 35
Phrik Pon Khua (Toasted-chile powder), 233
Pineapple
BBQ (Thai-style barbecue beef skewers), 137–38
Plaa Lek Thawt Krob (Fried tiny fish), 23–25
Plaa Meuk Ping (Grilled dried cuttlefish), 32–33
Pork
Aep Samoeng Muu (Pig's brains grilled in banana leaf), 141–43
Hang Muu Yaang (Grilled pig's tails), 144–46
Huu Muu Thawt (Fried pig's ears), 84–85
Jin Som Mok Khai (Sour pork and egg grilled in banana leaves), 158–60
Jok (Rice porridge), 217–18
Khaep Muu (Pork cracklings), 107–8
Khao Tom (Rice soup), 214–15
Laap Muu Thawt (Fried minced pork patties), 79–81
Laap Phrae (Phrae-style minced pork "salad"), 192–97
Muu Daet Diaw (Fried semidried pork), 91–92
Muu Deng (Bouncy pork balls), 246
Muu Ping (Grilled pork skewers), 226–27
Muu Yaang Thawt (Fried grilled pork), 115–16
Naem Sii Khrong Muu (Fried sour pork ribs), 109–13
roll, Vietnamese, 177
Sai Krawk Isaan (Isaan fermented pork-and-rice sausages), 147–50
Sai Muu Thawt (Fried chitterlings), 84–85
Sii Khrong Muu Tai Naam (Pork ribs cooked "underwater"), 124–25
Sup Kraduuk Muu (Thai Pork stock), 241–42
Tap Waan (Isaan pork liver salad), 187
Tom Leuat Muu (Pork soup with steamed blood cakes and offal), 219–21
Tom Saep Muu (Isaan sour soup with pork), 52–55
Yam Het Huu Nuu Khao (Mouse ear mushroom salad), 184–85
Yam Mama (Instant-noodle salad), 180–81
Yam Wun Sen (Glass noodle salad), 177–79
Porridge
Jok (Rice porridge), 217–18
Prawns
Kung Phao (Grilled prawns), 157

R

Radish, salted, 253
Rice
Jin Som Mok Khai (Sour pork and egg grilled in banana leaves), 158–60
Jok (Rice porridge), 217–18
Khao Hom Mali (Jasmine rice), 247

Rice, (continued)

Khao Khua (Toasted–sticky rice powder), 232

Khao Niaw (Sticky rice), 248–49

Khao Tom (Rice soup), 214–15

Sai Krawk Isaan (Isaan fermented pork-and-rice sausages), 147–50

Rice steamer set, sticky, 257

Rice whiskey

Lao Khao (Rice whiskey), 11–17

Ya Dawng (Herbal rice whiskey), 40

S

Sai Krawk Isaan (Isaan fermented pork-and-rice sausages), 147–50

Sai Muu Thawt (Fried chitterlings), 84–85

Salads

Laap Neua Dip (Nan-style minced raw beef "salad"), 188–91

Laap Phrae (Phrae-style minced pork "salad"), 192–97

Som Tam Thawt (Fried papaya salad), 101–3

Sup Naw Mai (Isaan bamboo shoot salad), 166–69

Tap Waan (Isaan pork liver salad), 187

Yam Het Huu Nuu Khao (Mouse ear mushroom salad), 184–85

Yam Mama (Instant-noodle salad), 180–81

Yam Plaa Meuk (Squid salad), 172–73

Yam Plaa Salit (Fried gouramy fish salad), 174–76

Yam Wun Sen (Glass noodle salad), 177–79

Sausages

Mam (Isaan beef and liver sausage), 117–21

Sai Krawk Isaan (Isaan fermented pork-and-rice sausages), 147–50

Sawtooth herb, 253

Scales, 257

Seasoning sauce, 254

Shallots

Asian, 254

Hom Jiaw (Fried shallots), 235

Naam Man Hom Jiaw (Shallot oil), 235

Shaoxing wine, 254

Shrimp

Kapi Kung (Homemade shrimp paste), 238

Kung Haeng Khua (Dry-fried dried shrimp), 239

Kung Ten (Dancing shrimp), 29–30

live, 30

Yam Mama (Instant-noodle salad), 180–81

See also Prawns

Sichuan peppercorns, black, 252

Sii Khrong Muu Tai Naam (Pork ribs cooked "underwater"), 124–25

Silver fungus. See White fungus

Skewers

BBQ (Thai-style barbecue beef skewers), 137–38

Muu Ping (Grilled pork skewers), 226–27

Tap Kai Ping (Grilled chicken liver skewers), 153–55

Tap Pet Ping (Grilled duck liver skewers), 153–55

Snow fungus. See White fungus

Som Tam Thawt (Fried papaya salad), 101–3

Soups

Kaeng Awm (Northern Thai stewed beef), 45–47

Khao Tom (Rice soup), 214–15

Kuaytiaw Luuk Chin Plaa Hua Nom (Noodle soup with tiny fish balls), 223–24

Tom Leuat Muu (Pork soup with steamed blood cakes and offal), 219–21

Tom Saep Muu (Isaan sour soup with pork), 52–55

Yam Kop (Northern Thai frog soup), 49–51

Soy sauce, types of, 254

Spider skimmers, 257

Squid

Yam Plaa Meuk (Squid salad), 172–73

Stir-fries
  Khua Haem Pik Kai (Stir-fried chicken wings with hot basil and chiles), 205–8
  Phat Hoi Laai Samun Phrai (Stir-fried clams with krachai, galangal, and Thai basil), 209–11
  Phat Khii Mao (Drunkard's stir-fry), 201–4
  tips for, 199
Stock
  Sup Kraduuk Muu (Thai Pork stock), 241–42
Sup Naw Mai (Isaan bamboo shoot salad), 166–69

T

Tamarind, 254
  Naam Makham Piak (Tamarind water), 236
Tap Kai Ping (Grilled chicken liver skewers), 153–55
Tap Pet Ping (Grilled duck liver skewers), 153–55
Tap Waan (Isaan pork liver salad), 187
Thai basil, 254
Thua Thawt Samun Phrai (Fried peanuts with makrut lime leaves, garlic, and chiles), 26–28
Tomatillos
  Tom Som Kai Baan (Sour Northern Thai "village chicken" soup), 57–59
Tomatoes
  Som Tam Thawt (Fried papaya salad), 101–3
  Tom Som Kai Baan (Sour Northern Thai "village chicken" soup), 57–59
  Yam Het Huu Nuu Khao (Mouse ear mushroom salad), 184–85
  Yam Mama (Instant-noodle salad), 180–81
  Yam Plaa Meuk (Squid salad), 172–73
Tom Leuat Muu (Pork soup with steamed blood cakes and offal), 219–21
Tom Saep Muu (Isaan sour soup with pork), 52–55

Tom Som Kai Baan (Sour Northern Thai "village chicken" soup), 57–59
Turmeric root, yellow, 254

W

Whiskey, 162
  Lao Khao (Rice whiskey), 11–17
  soda, 162
  Ya Dawng (Herbal rice whiskey), 40
White fungus, 184, 185
  Yam Het Huu Nuu Khao (Mouse ear mushroom salad), 184–85
White pepper, 254
Woks, 199, 257
Wok spatulas, 257

Y

Ya Dawng (Herbal rice whiskey), 40
Yam Het Huu Nuu Khao (Mouse ear mushroom salad), 184–85
Yam Kop (Northern Thai frog soup), 49–51
Yam Mama (Instant-noodle salad), 180–81
Yam Met Mamuang Himaphaan (Fried cashews with salt, chiles, and green onions), 37–38
Yam Plaa Meuk (Squid salad), 172–73
Yam Plaa Salit (Fried gouramy fish salad), 174–76
Yam Wun Sen (Glass noodle salad), 177–79

Library of Congress Cataloging-in-Publication Data
is on file with the publisher.

Hardcover ISBN: 978-1-60774-773-4
eBook ISBN: 978-1-60774-774-1

Printed in China

Design by Kara Plikaitis
Cover design by makelike
Photo look and color by Adam Levey

10 9 8 7 6 5 4 3 2 1

First Edition